Knitting the Chill Away

39 Cozy Patterns for the Whole Family

Martingale®
Create with Confidence

Knitting the Chill Away:
39 Cozy Patterns for the Whole Family
© 2012 by Martingale®

Martingale
Create with Confidence

Martingale
19021 120th Ave. NE, Ste. 102
Bothell, WA 98011-9511 USA
ShopMartingale.com

Printed in China
17 16 15 14 13 12   8 7 6 5 4 3 2 1

Library of Congress Cataloging-in-Publication Data is available upon request.

ISBN: 978-1-60468-083-6

MISSION STATEMENT
*Dedicated to providing quality products
and service to inspire creativity.*

CREDITS
President & CEO: Tom Wierzbicki
Editor in Chief: Mary V. Green
Design Director: Paula Schlosser
Managing Editor: Karen Costello Soltys
Translator: Donna Druchunas
Technical Editor: Amy Polcyn
Copy Editor: Melissa Bryan
Production Manager: Regina Girard
Cover & Text Designer: Regina Girard
Illustrator: Adrienne Smitke
Photography: frechverlag GmbH, Stuttgart;
lighting by Michael Ruder, Stuttgart

The original German edition was published as *Winterträume Stricken*. Copyright ©2010 frechverlag GmbH, Stuttgart, Germany. This edition is published by arrangement with Claudia Böhme, Rights & Literary Agency, Hannover, Germany (www.agency-boehme.com).

Contents

Introduction

When we think of winter, we often envision severe cold and dreary, dark days. But this season has so much beauty to offer: sleigh rides in the sunshine, athletic snowball fights, and romantic walks in an enchanted landscape. After such a winter excursion, you can sit by a warm fireplace and relax with a cup of hot chocolate. And what better way to enjoy this cozy atmosphere than to get out your knitting and create unique magic to keep you warm on your next winter outing?

In this book, you'll find smart and beautiful projects for the whole family: from fashionable sweaters and patterned scarves, hats, and gloves to fluffy pillows and comfortable socks.

Find your favorite project and cast on. You'll see, winter will soon become your favorite season!

Let's Go Sledding

As soon as the first snowflakes dance merrily down from the sky, children of all ages sense the magic. In winter there's so much to do! Who builds the best snowman? Who catches the most snowflakes on their tongue? Who sleds the fastest? And then the first snowball flies by and a wild snowball fight with the whole family begins. The stylish and warm garments on the following pages will ensure that the cold doesn't spoil your fun.

Sugar and Spice

Skill level: Experienced ◼◼◼▷

Size: Girls' 4 (6, 8)

Finished chest: 27 (32, 34)"

Finished length: 13 (14¼, 15¾)", excluding fringe

MATERIALS

100% merino wool: 300 (350, 350) g/830 (965, 965) yds, color rose ③

Size 4 (3.5 mm) and 6 (4 mm) straight needles or size required to obtain gauge

Stitch markers

Cable needle

Tapestry needle

Package of 4.5 mm pony beads in assorted colors (approx 100)

Beading needle

GAUGE

Body: 29 sts and 34 rows = 4" with larger needles in chart B patt

Border: 19 sts and 40 rows = 2½" x 4" with smaller needles in chart A patt

CABLE PATTERNS

See charts A and B (page 9). **Note:** On chart B, work sts on WS rows as they appear.

BACK

Border

With smaller needles, CO 24 sts.

Work chart A until piece measures 27 (32, 34)". **Note:** When dropping the sts in row 7, it is easiest to drop all 7 sts tog, then cast on 7 sts to replace them at beg of next row using a cable cast on (see "Cable Cast On" on page 106). Dropped sts will be unraveled into fringe later.

Bind off.

Fold border in half and place a marker at the fold line to separate front and back. Be sure to orient border so that the cable is at the top and the side to be unraveled into fringe is at the bottom.

Body

With RS facing and larger needles, PU 100 (118, 130) sts along half of the top edge of border (from right edge to the marker).

Row 1 (WS): Purl.

Beg working chart B as foll:

Row 1 (RS): K1 (selvage), K0 (3, 2), PM, work 26-st rep of chart B beg with st 7 (1, 7) once; work 26-st rep 3 (3, 4) more times, work last 6 sts of chart 0 (1, 0) times, PM, K0 (3, 2), K1 (selvage).

Row 2 (WS): K1 (selvage), P0 (3, 2), slip marker, work chart B as set to next marker, slip marker, P0 (3, 2), K1 (selvage).

Cont working patt as est until piece measures 10¼ (11½, 13)" from border. End after a WS row.

Shape Neck

Next row (RS): BO center 30 (36, 42) sts.

Working both shoulders separately, BO 3 sts each neck edge once, then BO 2 sts each neck edge once—30 (36, 39) sts each shoulder.

Work even until piece measures 11 (12¼, 13¾)" from border.

BO rem sts, working K2tog at center of each 6-st cable.

FRONT

PU 100 (118, 130) sts from marker to left edge of border and work as for back until piece measures 8¼ (9½, 11)" from border.

End after a WS row.

Shape Neck

Next row (RS): BO center 14 (20, 26) sts.

Working both shoulders separately, BO 4 sts each neck edge, then BO 2 sts each neck edge 3 times, then BO 1 st each neck edge 3 times—30 (36, 39) sts each shoulder.

When front measures same as back, BO rem sts, working K2tog at center of each 6-st cable.

SLEEVES

Cuff

Border (without fringe)

With smaller needles, CO 19 sts. Beg working chart A, omitting fringe sts (work even in patt as set to end of row), until piece measures 6½ (7, 7)".

Bind off.

Arm

With RS facing and larger needles, PU 48 (54, 54) sts along top edge of border.

Purl 1 row (WS).

Beg working chart B as foll:

Row 1 (RS): K1 (selvage), beg with st 7 (1, 1) of chart, work 26-st rep of chart B once, work 26-st rep once more, work last 6 sts of chart 0 (1, 1) times, K1 (selvage).

Cont working patt as est and AT THE SAME TIME, after completing 3 rows, beg sleeve shaping as foll:

On next and every 4th row, inc 1 st each end of row 7 (12, 16) times, then every other row inc 1 st each end of row 16 (11, 11) times—94 (100, 108) sts.

Work even until sleeve measures 7½ (8½, 10¼)" from border. BO.

FINISHING

Weave in ends. Wash and lay flat to dry.

Sew shoulder seams.

Pin center of each sleeve to body at shoulder seam and sew in sleeves.

Sew underarm seams and then side seams, stopping above fringe sts.

Neckband

With smaller needles, CO 12 sts.

Set up patt as foll:

Row 1 (RS): K3, PM, work sts 11–16 of chart A, PM, K3.

Cont in patt as est, working garter st on outside edges and chart A between markers until piece measures 16¾ (17¼, 19)".

Bind off.

Starting at left shoulder, sew the border around neck opening. Sew CO to BO edge of border at left shoulder.

At lower edge of body, unravel dropped sts into fringe, cutting loops open at bottom.

Fringe

String beads as desired, tying overhand knots to hold in place.

Cable chart A (border pattern)

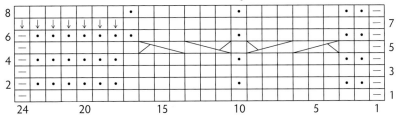

Repeat = 24 sts

Cable chart B (body pattern)

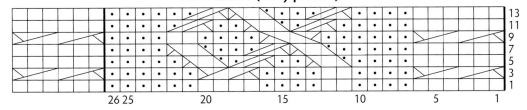

Repeat = 26 sts

Chart Legend

☐ K on RS, P on WS

• P on RS, K on WS

— Selvage st

↓ Drop st and allow to unravel, CO new st

◫ Sl 2 to cn and hold in front, P1, K2 from cn

◫ Sl 1 to cn and hold in back, K2, P1 from cn

◫ Sl 2 to cn and hold in front, K2, K2, from cn

◫ Sl 2 to cn and hold in back, K2, K2, from cn

◫ Sl 3 to cn and hold in back, K3, K3 from cn

◫ Sl 3 to cn and hold in front, K3, K3, from cn

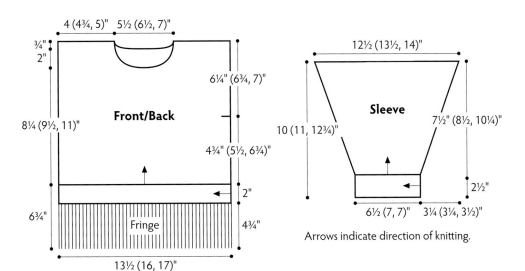

Arrows indicate direction of knitting.

Heart and Soul

Men's Pullover

Skill level: Easy ◼◼☐☐
Size: Men's Small (Medium, Large)
Finished chest: 40 (46, 49)"
Finished length: 27¼ (27¼, 27¼)"

MATERIALS

100% merino wool: 900 (950, 1000) g/1585 (1675, 1760) yds, color beige heather (5)
Size 8 (5 mm) straight needles or size required to obtain gauge
Size 6 (4 mm) 16" circular needle for neckband
Stitch markers
Cable needle
Tapestry needle

GAUGE

23 sts and 23 rows = 4" with larger needles in cable patt

PATTERN STITCHES

Cable

See chart (page 12). **Note:** Work sts on WS rows as they appear.

Ribbing

Multiple of 2 sts
All rnds: (K1, P1) around.

BACK

With larger needles, CO 120 (133, 146) sts and purl 1 row. Set up cable pattern as foll:

Row 1 (RS): K1 (selvage), PM, work 13-st cable rep 9 (10, 11) times, work last st of chart, PM, K1 (selvage).

Cont in patt as est, knitting first and last st of every row and working cable patt between markers, until piece measures 17¾ (17, 17)". End after a WS row.

Shape Armhole

BO 4 sts at beg of next 2 rows, then BO 2 sts at beg of next 2 rows 3 (3, 4) times, then dec 1 st each end of every RS row 3 (3, 5) times—94 (107, 112) sts rem. Work even until piece measures 26½". End after a WS row.

Shape Shoulders and Neck

BO 8 (9, 8) sts at beg of next 2 rows, then BO 7 (8, 9) sts at beg of next 2 rows 3 times. AT THE SAME TIME, after first 2 rows of shoulder shaping, BO center 30 (35, 36) sts, then working both sides separately, dec 1 st each neck edge 3 times—all sts consumed.

FRONT

Work as for back until piece measures 24". End after a WS row.

Shape Neck and Shoulders

On next row, BO center 12 (17, 18) sts, then working each side separately, BO 3 sts each neck edge once, then BO 2 sts each neck edge 3 times, then dec 1 st each end of next RS row 3 times—29 (33, 35) sts each shoulder. AT THE SAME TIME, when front measures same as back to shoulders, shape shoulders as for back.

SLEEVES

With larger needles, CO 55 (68, 68) sts and purl 1 row.

Work in cable patt, knitting first and last st of every row for selvage sts as before. On the 14th row, inc 1 st each end of row, then inc 1 st each end of row every 6th row 6 times, then every 4th row 10 times, then every other row 6 times—101 (114, 114) sts.

Work even until piece measures 18". End after a WS row.

Shape Cap

BO 4 sts at beg of next 2 rows, BO 2 sts at beg of next 2 rows 3 times, then dec 1 st each end of every RS row 4 times, then BO 2 sts at beg of next 2 rows 6 times, then BO 3 sts 3 times, then BO 5 sts once. BO rem 21 (34, 34) sts.

FINISHING

Weave in ends. Wash and lay flat to dry.

Sew shoulder seams.

Pin center of each sleeve to body at shoulder seam and sew in sleeves.

Sew side seams and underarm seams.

Neckband

With circular needle, RS facing, PU 76 (86, 86) sts around neck opening starting at left shoulder, PM. Working in the round, work in ribbing until collar measures 8". BO loosely in patt. Fold collar in half to outside.

Cable chart

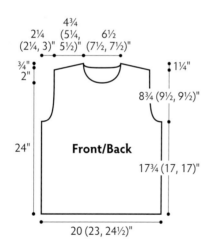

Repeat = 13 sts

⬜ K on RS, P on WS

⊡ P on RS, K on WS

◨ Sl 1 to cn and hold in back, K2, K1 from cn

◧ Sl 1 to cn and hold in front, K2, K1 from cn

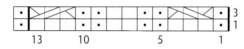

Boy's Pullover

Skill level: Easy ◼◼◻◻

Size: Boys' 6 (8, 10)

Finished chest: 28 (32, 35)"

Finished length: 15¾ (17¼, 18¾)"

MATERIALS

100% merino wool: 350 (350, 400) g/965 (965, 1105) yds, color indigo [3]

Size 4 (3.5 mm) straight needles or size required to obtain gauge

Size 4 (3.5 mm) 16" circular needle for neckband

Stitch markers

Cable needle

Tapestry needle

Front/Back (schematic)

4¾
2¼ (5¼, 6½
(2¼, 3)" 5½)" (7½, 7½)"

¾"
2"

1¼"

8¾ (9½, 9½)"

24"

17¾ (17, 17)"

20 (23, 24½)"

Sleeve (schematic)

17 (19, 19)"

6¼"

24½"

18"

4" 9 (11, 11)"

GAUGE

29 sts and 32 rows = 4" (10 cm) with larger needles in cable patt

PATTERN STITCHES

Cable

See chart for men's pullover (page 12). Work sts on WS rows as they appear.

Ribbing

Multiple of 2 sts
All rnds: (K1, P1) around.

BACK

CO 107 (120, 133) sts and purl 1 row.

Set up charted patt as foll:

Row 1 (RS): K1 (selvage), PM, work 13-st cable rep 8 (9, 10) times, work last st of chart, PM, K1 (selvage).

Cont in patt as est, knitting first and last st of every row and working cable patt between markers, until piece measures 9 (9¾, 10½)". End after a WS row.

Shape Armhole

BO 8 sts at beg of next 2 rows—91 (104, 117) sts rem.

When piece measures 15¾ (17½, 19)", BO all sts.

FRONT

Work as for back until piece measures 13¾ (15½, 17)". End after a WS row.

Shape Neck

On next row, BO center 13 (18, 27) sts, then working shoulders separately, BO 4 sts each neck edge once, then BO 2 sts each neck edge twice, then dec 1 st each neck edge 3 times—28 (32, 34) sts. AT THE SAME TIME, when piece measures same as back, BO rem sts.

SLEEVES

CO 42 (55, 55) sts and purl 1 row.

Work in cable patt, knitting first and last st of every row for selvage sts as before. On the 4th row, inc 1st each end of row, then inc 1 st each end of row every 4th row 13 (20, 21) times, then every other row 15 (8, 12) times—100 (113, 123) sts.

Work even until sleeve measures 12 (13½, 15)". BO.

FINISHING

Weave in ends. Wash and lay flat to dry.

Sew shoulder seams.

Pin center of each sleeve to body at shoulder seam and sew in sleeves.

Sew side seams and underarm seams.

Neckband

With circular needle, RS facing, PU 80 (90, 102) sts around neck opening starting at left shoulder, PM. Working in the round, work in ribbing until collar measures 5½". BO loosely in patt. Fold collar in half to outside.

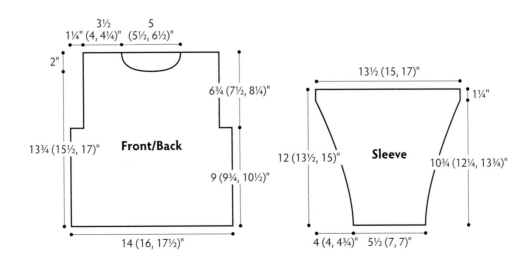

Color in the Snow

Women's Pullover

Skill level: Easy ◼◼◻◻

Size: Women's Medium (Large)

Finished bust: 38 (45½)"

Finished length: 19½ (21½)"

MATERIALS

Acrylic/wool blend: 700 (750) g/840 (900) yds, color chocolate (6)

Size 11 (8 mm) straight needles or size required to obtain gauge

Size 11 (8 mm) and 13 (9 mm) 16" circular needles

Stitch markers

Cable needle

Tapestry needle

GAUGE

14 sts and 18 rows = 4" with smaller needles in cable patt

PATTERN STITCHES

Ribbing

Multiple of 4 sts

All rnds: (K2, P2) around.

Cable

See chart (page 16). **Note:** Work sts on WS rows as they appear.

BODY

This sweater is made in one piece starting at the bottom front edge, going up and over the shoulders, ending with the bottom back edge.

Lower Front

With smaller needles, CO 70 (83) sts.

Set up row (WS): K1 (selvage), PM, P3, *K2, P6, K2, P3; rep from * to last st, PM, K1 (selvage).

Beg working cable patt between markers, ending with P3 and knitting first and last st of row for selvage sts.

Work even until piece measures 12½ (13½)". End after a WS row.

Upper Front and Sleeves

CO 65 sts at beg of next 2 rows (see "Cable Cast On," page 106) while cont to work in patt as est—200 (213) sts.

Work even until piece measures 17¾ (19¼)". End after a WS row.

Neck Opening

On next row BO center 14 (17) sts, then working both sides separately, BO 3 sts each neck edge once, then BO 2 sts each neck edge once, then dec 1 st each neck edge every other row twice—86 (91) sts each side.

Work even until piece measures 19½ (21½)" and PM at neck edge on both sides to mark the shoulder line. Work 2 more rows, then on next row CO 28 (31) sts over neck opening—200 (213) sts.

Upper Back and Sleeves

Work even until piece measures 26½ (29½)". BO 65 sts at beg of next 2 rows—70 (83) sts rem for lower back.

Lower Back

Work even until when folded in half at shoulder line back measures same as front. BO.

FINISHING

Weave in ends. Wash and lay flat to dry.

Fold piece in half at shoulder line and sew underarm and side seams.

Neckband

With smaller circular needle, RS facing, PU 76 (84) sts at neck opening. PM and work in ribbing for 2", then change to larger needle and work even for another 2". BO loosely in patt. Fold collar in half to outside.

Cable chart

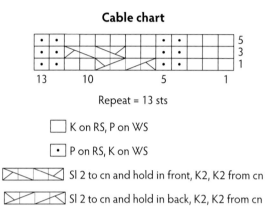

Repeat = 13 sts

⬜ K on RS, P on WS

⊡ P on RS, K on WS

◤�◥ Sl 2 to cn and hold in front, K2, K2 from cn

◣◥ Sl 2 to cn and hold in back, K2, K2 from cn

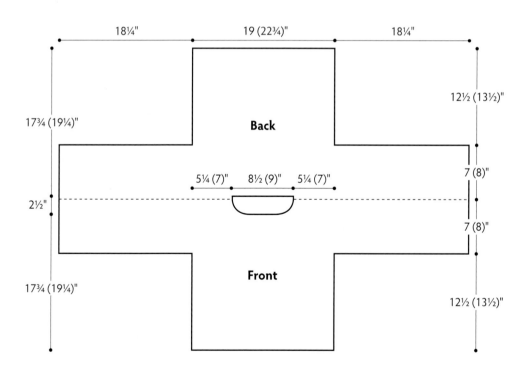

Girls' Pullover

Skill level: Easy ◑■☐☐

Size: Girls' 4 (8)

Finished chest: 24 (31)"

Finished length: 14½ (16½)"

MATERIALS

Acrylic/wool blend: 450 (500) g/540 (600) yds, color pink
🧶

Size 11 (8 mm) straight needles or size required to obtain gauge

Size 11 (8 mm) and 13 (9 mm) 16" circular needles

Stitch markers

Cable needle

Tapestry needle

GAUGE

14 sts and 18 rows = 4" with smaller needles in cable patt

PATTERN STITCHES

Ribbing

Multiple of 4 sts

All rnds: (K2, P2) around.

Cable

See chart (page 16). **Note:** Work sts on WS rows as they appear.

BODY

This sweater is made in one piece starting at the bottom front edge, going up and over the shoulders, ending with the bottom back edge.

Lower Front

With smaller needles, CO 44 (57) sts.

Work as for women's pullover until piece measures 9½ (10½"). End after a WS row.

Upper Front and Sleeves

CO 39 (52) sts at beg of next 2 rows (see "Cable Cast On," page 106) while cont to work in patt as est—122 (161) sts.

Work even until piece measures 12½ (14½)". End after a WS row.

Neck Opening

On next row BO center 8 (11) sts, then working both sides separately, BO 2 sts each neck edge twice, then dec 1 st each neck edge 1 (2) time—52 (69) sts each side.

Work even until piece measures 14½ (16½)" and PM at neck edge on both sides to mark the shoulder line. Work 2 more rows, then on next row CO 18 (23) sts over neck opening—122 (161) sts.

Upper Back and Sleeves

Work even until piece measures 19½ (22½)", then BO 39 (52) sts at beg of next 2 rows—44 (57) sts rem for lower back.

Lower Back

Work even until when folded in half at shoulder line back measures same as front. BO.

FINISHING

Weave in ends. Wash and lay flat to dry.

Fold piece in half at shoulder line and sew underarm and side seams.

Neckband

With smaller circular needle, RS facing, PU 48 (56) sts at neck opening. Work as for women's pullover.

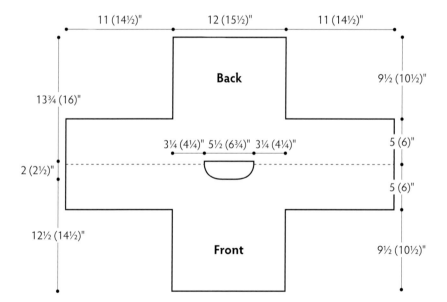

Color in the Snow

Hand in Hand in the Snow

Gradually, the densely falling snow transforms the landscape into a glittering fairyland. Silent and enchanted, the white winter wonderland creates the perfect mood for romantic walks hand in hand. Whether you prefer whispered declarations of love, cuddling against the cold, or a boisterous romp in the snow, with the garments in this section you'll both be kept warm.

Very Chic Gray on Gray

Skill level: Intermediate ◼◼◼◻

Size: One size

Finished circumference:

   Mittens: Approx 10½"

   Hat: Approx 21½"

MATERIALS

100% merino wool: 🧶3

   MC: 100 g/276 yds, color medium gray

   CC: 50 g/138 yds, color dark gray

Set of 5 size 4 (3.5 mm) double-pointed needles or size
   required to obtain gauge

Stitch markers

Cable needle

Tapestry needle

GAUGE

22 sts and 30 rows = 4" in St st

SPECIAL INSTRUCTIONS

C2B: Sl 1 st to cn and hold in back, K1, K1 from cn.

C2F: Sl 1 st to cn and hold in front, K1, K1 from cn.

PATTERN STITCHES

St st in the round

Knit every round.

Rev St st in the round

Purl every round.

Ribbing A

Multiple of 3 sts

All rnds: (P1, K1, P1) around.

Ribbing B

Multiple of 6 sts

All rnds: (P1, K4, P1) around.

Cable

Multiple of 12 sts

Note: Slip all sts purlwise.

Rnd 1: *P1, K4, P1; rep from * around.

Rnds 2–5: *P1, K1, sl 2, K1, P2, sl 1, K2, sl 1, P1; rep from
* around.

Rnd 6: *P1, C2B, C2F, P2, C2F, C2B, P1; rep from *
around.

Rnd 7: Rep rnd 1.

Rnds 8–11: *P1, sl 1, K2, sl 1, P2, K1, sl 2, K1, P1; rep
from * around.

Rnd 12: *P1, C2F, C2B, P2, C2B, C2F, P1; rep from *
around.

Rep rnds 1–12 for patt.

Mittens

LEFT MITTEN

With CC, CO 60 sts. Arrange sts evenly on 4 dpns and
join to work in the round, being careful not to twist sts
(see "Working with Double-Pointed Needles," page 110).

CUFF

Work in ribbing A for 1¼", then change to MC and
cont in ribbing A until cuff measures 2½". Change to
ribbing B.

HAND

When cuff measures 3", beg cable patt. When piece measures 4¾", cont working cable patt on needles 1 and 2, and change to rev St st on needles 3 and 4.

Next rnd: Dec 3 sts on each of needles 3 and 4—54 sts rem.

THUMB GUSSET

On needle 4, P10, PM, M1 pw, P1, M1 pw, PM, P1—2 sts inc.

*Work 2 rnds even.

Next rnd: Work in patt to marker, slip marker, M1 pw, purl to next marker, M1 pw, slip marker, work in patt to end.

Rep from * until there are 19 gusset sts.

Work 1 rnd even.

Next rnd: Put thumb gusset sts on holder or waste yarn and CO 5 sts over the thumb opening—58 sts.

Cont in patt as est, working the 5 new sts as foll:

Next rnd: P5.

Next rnd: P2tog tbl, P1, P2tog—56 sts.

Next rnd: P3.

Next rnd: P3tog—54 sts rem.

Work 30 rnds in patt as est.

FINGERTIPS

Change to CC and beg working rev St st on all needles.

Next rnd: Dec 3 sts on each of needles 3 and 4—48 sts rem.

Dec rnd: *P1, P2tog tbl, purl to end of needle; purl to last 3 sts on next needle, P2tog, P1; rep from * once more on needles 3 and 4—44 sts.

Next rnd: Purl.

Rep last 2 rnds until 36 sts rem, then rep dec rnd every rnd until 8 sts rem. Break yarn, run tail through rem sts, and pull gently to fasten off.

THUMB

Put 19 thumb sts onto dpns. Join MC and PU 4 sts over gap. Purl around, working these 3 sts tog on next rnd—21 sts rem.

Work even in rev St st for 15 rnds.

Next rnd: (P1, P2tog) around—14 sts.

Next rnd: Purl.

Next rnd: (P2tog) around—7 sts.

Break yarn, run tail through rem sts, and pull gently to fasten off.

Weave in ends.

RIGHT MITTEN

Work as for left mitten to start of thumb gusset.

THUMB GUSSET

On needle 3, p1, PM, M1 pw, p1, M1 pw, PM, work to end of rnd—2 sts inc. *Work 2 rnds even.

Next rnd: Work in patt to marker, slip marker, M1 pw, purl to next marker, M1 pw, slip marker, work in patt to end.

Rep from * until there are 19 gusset sts.

Work 1 rnd even.

On the next rnd, put the thumb gusset sts on hold and CO 5 sts over the thumb opening—58 sts. Finish as for left mitten.

Hat

With CC, CO 120 sts. Arrange sts evenly on 4 dpns and join to work in the round, being careful not to twist sts. Work in ribbing A for ¾", then change to MC and cont in ribbing A until cuff measures 1½". Change to ribbing B. When cuff measures 2", beg cable patt.

CROWN

When hat measures 8", PM after every 10 sts and change to St st.

Dec rnd: (K8, K2tog) around—108 sts.

Next rnd: Knit.

Dec rnd: (K7, K2tog) around—96 sts.

Cont dec in this manner, working K2tog before each marker, until 12 sts rem.

Next rnd: (K2tog) around—6 sts.

Break yarn, run tail through rem sts, and pull gently to fasten off.

Weave in ends.

All-Occasion Bolero

Size: Women's Medium (Large)

Finished bust: 38 (41)"

Finished length: 16½ (16½)"

MATERIALS

100% merino wool: 500 (500) g/1380 (1380) yds, color gray heather ⓷

Size 7 (4.5 mm) and 8 (5 mm) 40" circular needles or size required to obtain gauge

Spare size 8 (5 mm) 40" circular needle

Stitch markers

Cable needle

Tapestry needle

GAUGE

20 sts and 24 rows = 4" with larger needles in texture patt

PATTERN STITCHES

Ribbing

Multiple of 2+1 sts

Row 1 (RS): K1, (P1, K1) across.

Row 2: Work sts as they appear.

Work rows 1 and 2 for patt.

Texture

Multiple of 4+2 sts

Row 1 (RS): (P1, K3) to last 2 sts, P1, K1.

Rows 2 and 3: Work sts as they appear.

Row 4: P1, K1, (YO, P3tog, YO, K1) to end.

Row 5: P1, K1, (P1, K3) to end.

Rows 6 and 7: Work sts as they appear.

Row 8: (YO, P3tog, YO, K1), to last 2 sts, P1, K1.

Rep rows 1–8 for patt.

NOTE

This bolero is worked in one piece, beginning with left front.

Left Front

With larger needles, CO 48 (52) sts and knit 2 rows.

Next row (RS): K1 (selvage), work in texture patt to last st, K1 (selvage). Cont in patt as set for 4", knitting first and last st of each row for selvage sts. End after a WS row. Beg inc for the sleeve on the right edge as foll:

Using the cable CO (see page 106), CO 4 sts at beg of every 4th row 6 times. Then CO 4 sts at beg of EOR 6 times, working inc into texture patt—96 (100) sts.

Work 1 row even, then in the next row, CO 16 sts at beg of row—112 (116) sts.

Work even until piece measures 16½" from beg. PM at beg and end of this row to mark the shoulder line. End after a WS row.

Put sts on spare needle and set aside.

Right Front

Work as for left front to beg of sleeve shaping. End after a RS row. Beg inc for the sleeve on the left edge as foll:

Every 4th row (WS), CO 4 sts (see "Cable Cast On," page 106) at beg of row 6 times, then every other row CO 4 sts at beg of row 6 times, working inc into texture patt—96 (100) sts.

Work 1 row even, then in the next row, CO 16 sts at beg of row—112 (116) sts.

Back

Next row (RS): Return sts for left front to working needle. Maintaining texture patt, work across all sts on left and right front to join for back—224 (232) sts.

Work even until sleeve cuff measures 6¼" from shoulder line marker.

BO 16 sts at beg of next 2 rows, then BO 4 sts at beg of next 2 rows 6 times, then (work 2 rows even then BO 4 sts at beg of next 2 rows) 6 times—96 (104) sts rem.

Work even until back measures same as front from shoulder line marker to bottom edge.

BO.

FINISHING

Weave in ends. Wash and lay flat to dry.

Fold piece in half at shoulder line. Sew underarm and side seams.

Front Bands and Ties

With smaller circular needle, RS facing, CO 28 sts for tie, PU 201 sts around front openings, CO 28 sts for opposite tie—257 sts.

Work in ribbing for 1½". BO loosely in patt.

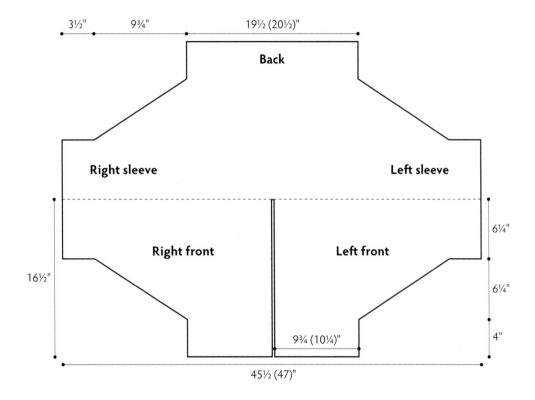

Wintertime by the Sea

Skill level: Intermediate ■■■□

Size: Men's Small (Medium, Large)

Finished chest: 40 (44, 48)"

Finished length: 26 (26, 26)"

MATERIALS

100% alpaca: 700 (750, 800) g/1525 (1635, 1744) yds, color blue heather ❸

Size 6 (4 mm) straight needles or size required to obtain gauge

Set of 5 size 4 (3.5 mm) double-pointed needles

Stitch markers

2 stitch holders

Cable needle

Tapestry needle

GAUGE

25 sts and 28 rows = 4" with larger needles in ribbing patt

65 sts of cable panel = 8" with larger needles

PATTERN STITCHES

Ribbing

Multiple of 4 sts

Row 1 (RS): (P1, K3) across.

Row 2: Work sts as they appear.

Rep rows 1 and 2 for patt.

Cable

See chart (page 29). **Note:** Work sts on WS rows as they appear.

BACK

With larger needles, CO 129 (141, 149) sts.

Row 1 (RS): K1 (selvage), K1, work in ribbing to last 3 sts, P1, K1, K1 (selvage).

Cont in ribbing until piece measures 17¼ (16½, 15¾)". End after a WS row.

Shape Armholes

BO 5 sts at beg of next 2 rows, then every other row dec 1 st each end of row 8 times—103 (115, 123) sts.

Final dec row (RS): K1 (selvage), K2, ssk, work in patt to last 5 sts, K2tog, K2, K1 (selvage)—101 (113, 121) sts.

Work even until piece measures 25¼". End after a WS row.

Shape Neck

Next row (RS): Put center 35 (39, 39) sts on hold. Working each shoulder separately, BO 3 (2, 3) sts each neck edge once, then BO 1 st each neck edge once—29 (34, 37) sts each shoulder. Work even until piece measures 26". BO.

FRONT

With larger needle, CO 141 (157, 165) sts and work in ribbing as for back.

When piece measures 2½", set up cable patt as foll:

Set up row (RS): K1 (selvage), work next 37 (45, 49) sts in rib patt as est, PM, work cable panel over next 65 sts, PM, work to last st in rib patt as est, K1 (selvage). Work even in patt as set, knitting first and last st of each row for selvage sts until piece measures same as back to armholes.

Shape Armholes

Work as for back—113 (129, 137) sts.

Work even until piece measures 22¾". End after a WS row.

Shape Neck

On next row put center 35 (37, 39) sts on hold, then working each shoulder separately, BO 3 sts at each neck edge once, then BO 2 sts each neck edge twice, then dec 1 st at each neck edge 3 (5, 5) times—29 (34, 37) sts each shoulder.

When piece measures same as back, BO rem sts.

SLEEVES

With larger needle, CO 53 (65, 69) sts and work in ribbing as for back, knitting first and last st of each row for selvage sts.

For sizes Small and Medium: Every 6th row, inc 1 st at each end of row 5 times, then alternating every 4th and 6th row, inc 1 st at each end of row 21 times—105 (117) sts. Work even until piece measures 19½". End after a WS row.

For size Large: Alternating every 4th and 6th row, inc 1 st at each end of row 20 times, then every 4th row inc 1 st at each end of row 9 times—127 sts. Work even until piece measures 19½". End after a WS row.

Shape Cap

BO 4 sts at beg of next 2 rows 9 times—33 (45, 55) sts rem.

When piece measures 22", BO.

FINISHING

Weave in ends. Wash and lay flat to dry.

Sew shoulder seams.

Pin center of each sleeve to body at shoulder seam and sew in sleeves.

Sew side seams and underarm seams.

Neckband

With smaller circular needle, RS facing, work across 35 (39, 39) held back neck sts, PU 29 (32, 33) sts, work across 35 (37, 39) held front neck sts, PU 29 (32, 33) sts—128 (140, 144) sts total.

PM and work in ribbing for 1½". BO loosely in patt.

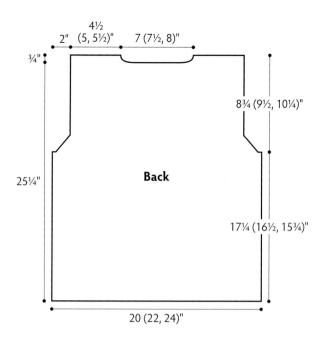

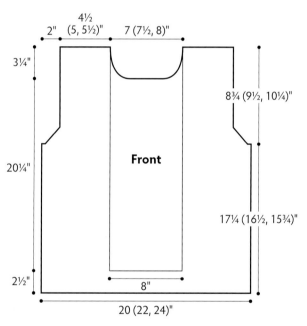

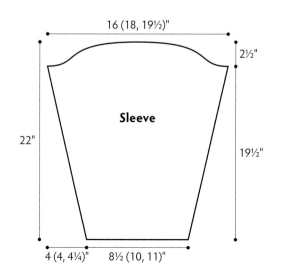

Cable chart and legend

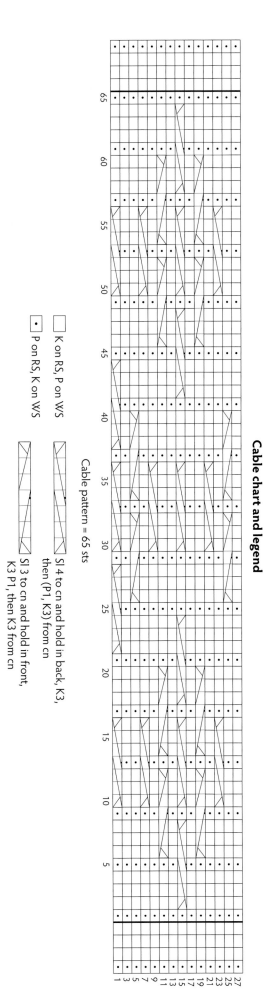

K on RS, P on WS

• P on RS, K on WS

Cable pattern = 65 sts

Sl 4 to cn and hold in back, K3,
then (P1, K3) from cn

Sl 3 to cn and hold in front,
K3 P1, then K3 from cn

Starry Skies

Skill level: Intermediate ■■■☐

Size: One size

Finished measurements:

Scarf: 9" x 71"

Hat: 21" circumference

MATERIALS

100% merino wool: 🧶5

For scarf:

A: 200 g/350 yds, color dark gray heather

B: 50 g/88 yds, color beige heather

C: 50 g/88 yds, color olive heather

For hat:

A: 100 g/175 yds, color dark gray heather

B: 50 g/88 yds, color beige heather

C: 50 g/88 yds, color olive heather

Size 8 (5 mm) straight needles for scarf or size required
to obtain gauge

Set of 5 size 6 (4 mm) and 8 (5 mm) double-pointed
needles for hat

Stitch markers

Tapestry needle

GAUGE

19 sts and 25 rows = 4" with larger needles in
colorwork patt

PATTERN STITCHES

St st in rows

RS: Knit all sts.

WS: Purl all sts.

St st in the round

Knit every rnd.

Ribbing in rows

Multiple of 2+1 sts

Row 1 (RS): K1, (P1, K1) across.

Row 2: Work sts as they appear.

Rep rows 1 and 2 for patt.

Ribbing in the round

Multiple of 2 sts

All rnds: (K1, P1) around.

Colorwork

See chart (page 32).

Scarf

With A, CO 43 sts and work 4 rows in ribbing.

Next row (WS): Knit.

Beg with last st of colorwork chart, work 20-st rep twice
in St st, end with first 2 sts of chart (see "Stranded
Colorwork," page 110).

Work all rows of chart, then with A, purl next WS row,
then change to ribbing.

PM at beg of row when scarf measures 35½" long
(halfway point). Cont in ribbing until second half
measures same as first to beg of colorwork patt.
Work colorwork patt as for first half, end with 4 rows
ribbing. BO.

FINISHING

Weave in ends.

Hat

With smaller dpns and A, CO 100 sts and work 5 rnds in ribbing.

Next rnd: Change to larger dpns and purl.

Work all rows of colorwork chart in St st.

Next rnd: Change to A and knit.

Next rnd: Purl.

Change to ribbing and work even until hat measures 7".

CROWN

Next rnd: (Work 10 sts in rib, PM) around.

Dec rnd: (Work to marker, K2tog, slip marker) around—90 sts rem.

Rep dec rnd every other rnd 5 times, then every rnd 3 times—10 sts rem.

Next rnd: K2tog around—5 sts rem.

Break yarn, run tail through rem sts and pull gently to fasten off.

FINISHING

Weave in ends.

Colorwork chart

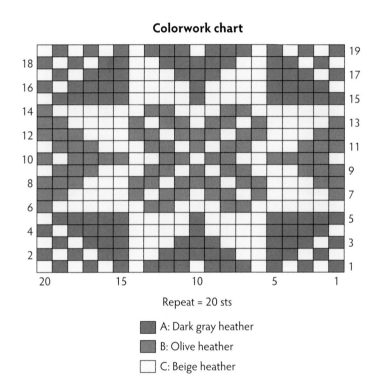

Repeat = 20 sts

■ A: Dark gray heather

■ B: Olive heather

□ C: Beige heather

Vintage-Inspired Turtleneck

Skill level: Experienced ◼◼◼◻

Size: Men's Medium (Large, Extra Large)

Finished chest: 42 (45, 48)"

Finished length: 26¾ (26¾, 27½)"

MATERIALS

100% alpaca: 750 (800, 850) g/1635 (1745, 1855) yds, color gray marble ④③

Size 4 (3.5 mm) and 6 (4 mm) straight needles or size required to obtain gauge

Size 4 (3.5 mm) 16" circular needle for neckband

Contrasting scrap yarn for provisional CO

Size E-4 (3.5 mm) crochet hook for provisional CO

Stitch markers

Cable needle

Tapestry needle

GAUGE

20 sts and 28 rows = 4" with larger needles in texture patt

28 sts of cable patt = 3½" wide with larger needles

PATTERN STITCHES

Ribbing in rows

Multiple of 2+1 sts

Row 1: K1, (P1, K1) across.

Row 2: Work sts as they appear.

Rep rows 1 and 2 for patt.

Ribbing in the round

Multiple of 2 sts

All rnds: (K1, P1) around.

Texture

See charts A and B (page 36). **Note:** Work sts on WS rows as they appear.

Cable

See chart (page 36). **Note:** Work sts on WS rows as they appear.

TUBULAR CAST ON

Pieces are cast on using the tubular method. Approximately half of the stitches are cast on provisionally (see page 107), and then increased to the total amount in the first row. When scrap yarn is removed, the hem will have a smooth edge that curves around to the wrong side.

BACK

With smaller needle and scrap yarn, CO 56 (60, 63) sts using a provisional method (see "Provisional Cast On," page 107).

Change to MC.

Row 1 (RS): K1 (selvage), (K1, YO) to last st, K1 (selvage)—110 (118, 124) sts.

Rows 2–4: K1, (K1, sl 1 pw wyif) to last st, K1.

Work in ribbing, knitting first and last st of each row for selvage for 3¼". End after a RS row.

Next row (WS): Inc 28 (28, 30) sts evenly across—138 (146, 154) sts.

Change to larger needles.

Row 1 (RS): K1 (selvage), PM then:

- Beg with st 11 (7, 3) of chart, work 8 (12, 16) sts of chart A, PM,
- 28 sts of cable patt, PM,
- 18 sts of chart B, PM,
- 28 sts of cable patt, PM,
- 18 sts chart A, PM,
- 28 sts of cable patt, PM,
- Work 8 (12, 16) sts of chart B, PM,
- K1 (selvage).

Work even in patt until piece measures 16½". End after a WS row.

Shape Armholes

BO 3 (5, 5) sts at beg of next 2 rows, then BO 2 sts next 2 rows 1 (2, 2) time, then dec 1 st each end of row of every other row 3 times—122 (122, 130) sts.

Work even until piece measures 26 (26, 26¾)". End after a WS row.

Shape Shoulders and Neck

BO 6 (6, 10) sts at beg of next 2 rows, then BO 8 sts at beg of next 2 rows 4 times.

AT THE SAME TIME, after the first 2 shoulder dec, BO center 36 sts, then working each side separately, BO 3 sts each neck edge once and then BO 2 sts each neck edge once—all sts consumed.

FRONT

Work as for back until piece measures 23¼ (23¼, 24)". End after a WS row.

Shape Neck and Shoulders

On next row, BO center 24 sts, then working each side separately, on the next 4 rows dec 1 st each neck edge, then BO 4 sts each neck edge once, then BO 2 sts twice, then dec 1 st each neck edge once—38 (38, 42) sts each shoulder.

AT THE SAME TIME, when piece measures same as back to shoulders, shape shoulders as for back.

SLEEVES

With smaller needles and scrap yarn, CO 24 sts. Then inc to 46 sts as for back. Work in ribbing until cuff measures 3¼", then on next WS row inc 20 sts evenly across—66 sts. Change to larger needles.

Row 1 (RS): K1 (selvage), PM, then:

- Work 18 sts of chart A, PM,
- 28 sts of cable patt, PM,
- Work 18 sts of chart B, PM,
- K1 (selvage).

Cont in patt as est, knitting first and last st of each row for selvage sts and AT THE SAME TIME, on row 6 and every foll 6th row, inc 1 at each end 18 (18, 14) times then inc every 4th row 0 (0, 8) times—102 (102, 110) sts. Work all inc into charts A and B.

Work even until piece measures 20¼". End after a WS row.

Shape Cap

BO 3 sts at beg of next 2 rows, then BO 2 sts at beg of next 2 rows twice, then BO 1 st at beg of next 2 rows 3 times, then BO 2 sts at beg of next 2 rows 7 times, then BO 3 sts at beg of next 2 rows twice, then BO 4 sts at beg of next 2 rows twice—26 (26, 34) sts rem.

BO rem sts, working K2tog 4 times across center cable panel.

FINISHING

Weave in ends. Wash and lay flat to dry.

Sew shoulder seams.

Pin center of each sleeve to the body at shoulder seam and sew in sleeves.

Remove the scrap yarn from the provisional cast on, revealing the tubular edge.

Sew side seams and underarm seams.

Neckband

With circular needle, RS facing, PU 128 sts around neck opening. PM and work in ribbing for 8".

BO loosely in patt. Fold collar in half to outside.

Cable chart and legend

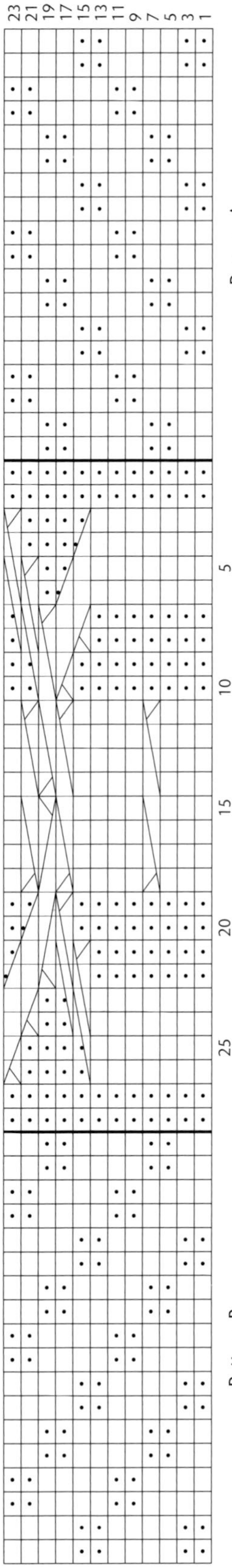

Pattern A
Pattern B

Cable pattern = 28 sts

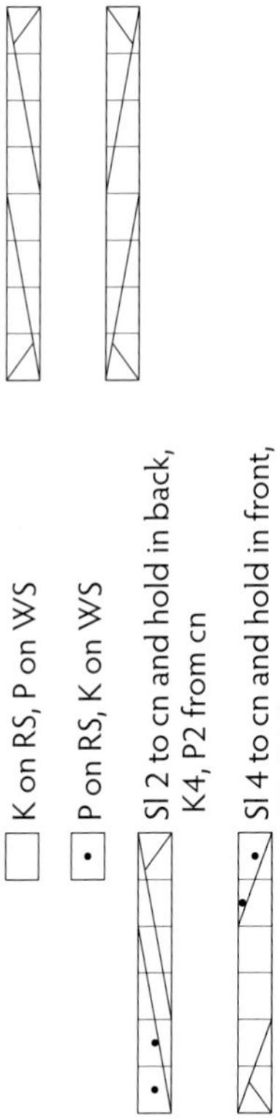

- K on RS, P on WS
- P on RS, K on WS
- Sl 2 to cn and hold in back, K4, P2 from cn
- Sl 4 to cn and hold in front, P2, K4 from cn
- Sl 4 to cn and hold in back, K4, K4 from cn
- Sl 4 to cn and hold in front, K4, K4 from cn

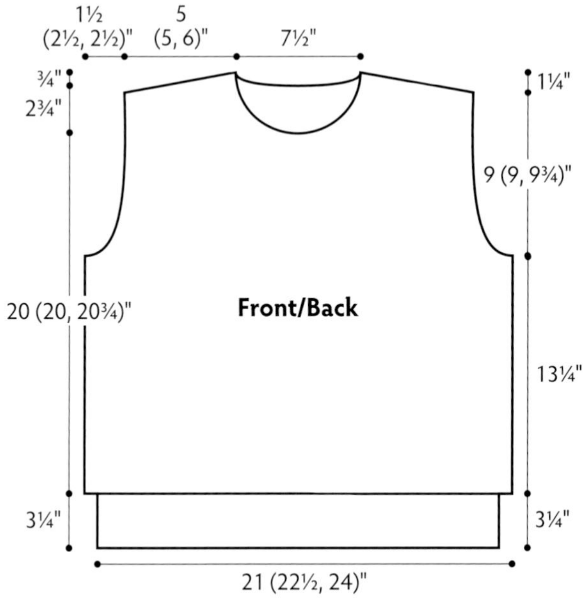

1½
(2½, 2½)"
5
(5, 6)"
7½"
¾"
2¾"
1¼"
9 (9, 9¾)"
20 (20, 20¾)"
Front/Back
13¼"
3¼"
3¼"
21 (22½, 24)"

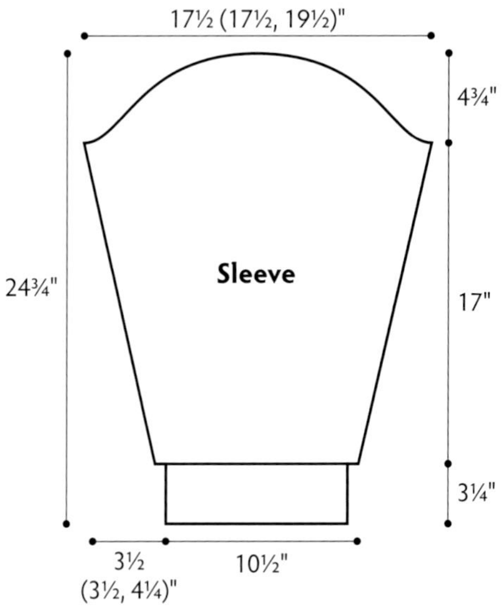

17½ (17½, 19½)"
4¾"
24¾"
Sleeve
17"
3¼"
3½
(3½, 4¼)"
10½"

Heart-Warming Cardigan

Skill level: Intermediate ■■■☐

Size: Women's Medium (Large, Extra Large)

Finished bust: 40¾ (42¼, 46¾)"

Finished length: 23¾ (24½, 25¼)"

MATERIALS

Wool/acrylic blend: 350 (400, 500) g/960 (1095, 1370) yds, color gray heather [3]

Size 6 (4 mm) and 8 (5 mm) straight needles or size required to obtain gauge

3 removable stitch markers or safety pins

Tapestry needle

3 anthracite buttons, approx 1½" diameter

Sewing needles and matching thread

GAUGE

19 sts and 24 rows = 4" with larger needles in fantasy st

PATTERN STITCHES

Ribbing

Multiple of 4+2 sts

Row 1 (RS): K2, (P2, K2) across.

Row 2: Work sts as they appear.

Rep rows 1 and 2 for patt.

Fantasy

Multiple of 3 sts

Row 1 (RS): Knit.

Rows 2 and 4: Purl.

Row 3: *Insert the needle from front to back into the second st 1 row below and pull up a loop, insert needle into second st 2 rows below and pull up a loop, K3 then pass the 2 loops over the 3 sts just knitted; rep from * across.

Rep rows 1–4 for patt.

BACK

With larger needles, CO 92 (98, 107) sts.

Row 1 (WS): K1 (selvage), purl to last st, K1 (selvage).

Work even in fantasy patt, knitting first and last st of each row for selvage sts, until piece measures 15¾" from beg. End after a WS row.

Shape Armhole

BO 5 sts at beg of next 2 rows, then BO 2 sts at beg of next 2 rows, then dec 1 st each end of row every other row twice—74 (80, 89) sts rem.

Work even until piece measures 23¾ (24½, 25¼)". BO.

LEFT FRONT

With larger needles, CO 44 (47, 53) sts.

Row 1 (WS): K1 (selvage), purl to last st, K1 (selvage).

Work even in fantasy patt with selvage sts until piece measures same as back to armhole. End after a WS row.

Shape Armhole

BO 5 sts at beg of next RS row, then BO 2 sts at beg of next RS row, then dec 1 st at beg of next RS row twice—35 (38, 44) sts. AT THE SAME TIME, when piece measures 15¾ (16½, 17¼)", beg neck shaping as foll:

Shape Neck

At beg of next WS row and on every foll WS row, dec 1 st 15 (15, 18) times—20 (23, 26) sts rem.

Work even until piece measures same as back. BO.

Button Band

With RS facing and smaller needles, PU 84 (88, 92) sts along center front.

Set up row (WS): K1 (selvage), P2, (K2, P2) across to last st, K1 (selvage).

Work even in ribbing, knitting first and last st for selvage sts until band measures 2¾". BO in patt.

RIGHT FRONT

Work as for left front to beg of armhole shaping, ending after a RS row.

Shape Armhole

BO 5 sts at beg of next WS row, then BO 2 sts at beg of next WS row, then dec 1 st at end of next RS row twice—35 (38, 44) sts. AT THE SAME TIME, when piece measures 15¾ (16½, 17¼)", beg neck shaping as foll:

Shape Neck

At beg of next RS row and on every following RS row, dec 1 st 15 (15, 18) times—20 (23, 26) sts rem. Work even until piece measures same as back. BO.

Buttonhole Band

On center, PM or safety pin 6 (6¾, 7½)" from bottom edge, and 2 more approx 4" apart to mark locations of buttonholes.

Work as for button band until band measures 1¼". End after a WS row.

Buttonhole row (RS): *Work in patt as est to marker, BO 4 sts; rep from * 2 more times, work in patt to end of row.

Next row (WS): Work in patt as est, CO 4 sts over each gap to finish buttonhole.

When band measures same as button band, BO in patt.

SLEEVES

With larger needles, CO 53 sts.

Row 1 (WS): K1 (selvage), purl to last st, K1 (selvage).

Work even in fantasy patt and AT THE SAME TIME, after working 19 (9, 7) rows, beg sleeve shaping as foll:

On the next RS row, inc 1 st at each end of row. Then inc 1 st each end of row every 8th row 4 times, then every 6th row 0 (4, 4) times, then every 4th row 6 (6, 10) times—75 (83, 91) sts.

Work even until piece measures 18". End after a WS row.

Shape Sleeve Cap

BO 5 sts at beg of next 2 rows, then BO 2 sts at beg of next 2 rows, then dec 1 st at each end of every RS row 12 times, then BO 2 sts at beg of next 2 rows twice, then BO 4 sts at beg of next 2 rows twice—13 (21, 29) sts. BO.

FINISHING

Weave in ends. Wash and lay flat to dry.

Sew shoulder seams.

Pin center of each sleeve to the body at shoulder seam and sew in sleeves. Sew side seams and underarm seams.

Collar

With smaller needles, RS facing, PU 176 (184, 192) sts around neck opening for collar. Work in ribbing patt for 6". BO loosely in patt. Sew buttons opposite buttonholes.

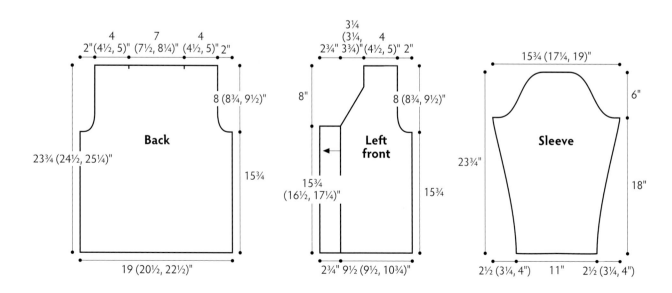

Easy Stripes

Skill level: Easy ◨■□▢

Size: One size

Finished measurements:

  Hat: Approx 23" circumference

  Scarf: 12" x 71"

MATERIALS

Acrylic/wool/alpaca blend: 🄖

100 g/130 yds each in:

  A: blue gray

  B: nut brown

  C: pink

  D: dark gray

  E: blue denim

Size 10½ (6.5 mm) straight needles or size required to
  obtain gauge

Tapestry needle

GAUGE

11 sts and 22 rows = 4" with larger needles in garter st

GARTER STITCH

Knit all rows.

Hat

Hat is worked flat in four identical segments shaped
with short rows, and seamed in back.

Stripe Pattern

Work 2 rows in each color in the following sequence:
*B, E, D, C, A, C, A, B, E, D, C, A, B; rep from * throughout.

With B, CO 28 sts. Working in garter st and stripe patt,
work short rows as foll:

Row 1 (RS): K26, turn.

Row 2 (and all WS rows): Sl 1, knit to end of row, turn.

Row 3: K24, turn.

Row 5: K22, turn.

Row 7: K20, turn.

Row 9: K18, turn.

Row 11: K16, turn.

Row 13: K14, turn.

Row 15: K12, turn.

Row 16: Rep row 2.

First half of segment is complete.

Row 17: K14, turn.

Row 19: K16, turn.

Row 21: K18, turn.

Row 23: K20, turn.

Row 25: K22, turn.

Row 27: K24, turn.

Row 29: K26, turn.

Row 31: Knit all sts, turn.

Row 32: Rep row 2.

Work rows 1–32 another 3 times. BO.

FINISHING

Sew back seam. Weave in ends.

Scarf

Scarf is worked sideways.

Work 2 rows in each color in the following sequence: *B, E, D, C, A; rep from * throughout. Cut the yarn after each row, and rejoin it leaving about 8" tails for fringe.

With B, CO 196 sts. Work in garter st rep stripe sequence until piece measures 12". BO.

FINISHING

To form fringe, tie an overhand knot in each group of 5 yarn tails across each end of the scarf.

Small on Texture, Big on Fit

Skill level: Intermediate ■■■□

Size: Men's Medium (Large, Extra Large)

Finished chest: 40 (45, 50½)"

Finished length: 26 (26¾, 27½)"

MATERIALS

Wool/acrylic blend: 800 (850, 900) g/2190 (2330, 2470) yds, color gray heather ③

Size 4 (3.5 mm) and 6 (4 mm) straight needles or size required to obtain gauge

Stitch markers

Cable needle

Tapestry needle

8 buttons, approx 1" diameter

Sewing needle and matching thread

GAUGE

30 sts and 30 rows = 4" with larger needles in cable patt

PATTERN STITCHES

Ribbing

Multiple of 2 sts

Row 1 (RS): (K1, P1) across.

Row 2: Work sts as they appear.

Rep rows 1 and 2 for patt.

Cable

See chart (page 45).

BACK

With smaller needle, CO 154 (174, 194) sts.

Row 1 (RS): K1 (selvage), (K1, P1) to last st, K1 (selvage).

Work in ribbing, knitting first and last st of each row for selvage sts until piece measures 3¼". End after a RS row.

Next row (WS): Work patt as est to last st, M1, K1—155 (175, 195) sts.

Change to larger needles and work in cable patt between selvage sts until piece measures 17½". End after a WS row.

Raglan Shaping

BO 10 sts at beg of next 2 rows—135 (155, 175) sts.

Set up for shaping (RS): K3, work in patt as est to last 3 sts, K3.

Cont in patt as est and dec at the beg and end of every RS row as foll:

Dec row 1: K2, ssk, work to last 4 sts, K2tog, K2—2 sts dec.

Next row: Work even.

Dec row 2: K2, sssk, work to last 5 sts, K3tog, K2—4 sts dec.

Next row: Work even.

Rep last 4 rows until 49 (59, 61) sts rem, a total of 29 (32, 38) dec rows.

Work even until piece measures 26 (26¾, 27½)". BO.

LEFT FRONT

With smaller needles, CO 74 (84, 94) sts and work in ribbing, knitting first and last st of each row for 3¼". Inc 1 st as for back on last row of ribbing—75 (85, 95) sts. With larger needle, work in cable patt between selvages until front measures same as back to beg of raglan shaping. End after a WS row.

Raglan Shaping

BO 10 sts at beg of next RS row, then working dec at beg of RS rows only for a total of 29 (32, 38) dec rows. AT THE SAME TIME, when piece measures 24½ (25¼, 26)", ending after a RS row, beg neck shaping as foll:

Shape Neck

At beg of WS rows, BO 6 (11, 12) sts once, 4 sts once, 3 sts once, and 2 sts 3 times. BO rem 3 sts.

RIGHT FRONT

Work as for left front to start of raglan shaping. End after a RS row.

Raglan Shaping

Work raglan shaping as for back, BO 10 sts at beg of next WS row, then working dec at beg of WS rows only for a total of 29 (32, 38) dec rows. AT THE SAME TIME, when piece measures 24½ (25¼, 26)", ending after a WS row, beg neck shaping as foll:

Shape Neck

At beg of RS rows, BO 6 (11, 12) sts once, 4 sts once, 3 sts once, and 2 sts 3 times. BO rem 3 sts.

SLEEVES

With smaller needles CO 74 (84, 84) sts and work in ribbing, knitting first and last st of each row for 3¼", inc 1 st on last row of ribbing as for back—75 (85, 85) sts. Change to larger needles and work in cable patt between selvages.

AT THE SAME TIME, inc 1 st at each end of row inside selvage sts as foll:

For sizes Medium and Large: Every 6th row 5 times, then every 4th row 19 times—123 (133) sts.

For size Extra Large: Every 4th row 18 times, then every other row 15 times—151 sts.

Work even until sleeve measures 18¼ (18¼, 17½)". End after a WS row.

Shape Cap

BO 10 sts at beg of next RS row, then working dec at each end of rows as for back for a total of 29 (32, 38) dec rows—17 sts. When sleeve measures 26¾ (27½, 27½)", BO rem sts.

FINISHING

Weave in ends. Wash and lay flat to dry.

Sew shoulder seams.

Pin center of each sleeve to the body at shoulder seam and sew in sleeves.

Sew side seams and underarm seams.

Neckband

With smaller needles, RS facing, PU 121 (127, 135) sts around neck opening and knit 1 row (WS).

Set up ribbing (RS): K1 (selvage), K1, (P1, K1) to last 2 sts, P1, K1 (selvage).

Work in patt as est until neckband measures 2¾". BO loosely in patt.

Button Band

On right front, with smaller needles and RS facing, PU 161 (165, 169) sts along center front including side of neckband and knit 1 row (WS). Set up ribbing as for neckband. When button band measures 2", BO loosely in patt.

Place markers on button band 1 (1½, 1)" from bottom edge, and 7 more spaced 3½ (3½, 4)" apart.

Buttonhole Band

Work as for button band until band measures 1". End after a WS row.

Next row (RS): BO 3 sts for each buttonhole, matching placement of markers on button band.

Next row: CO 3 sts over each gap to finish buttonhole, maintaining ribbing patt.

Work even until buttonhole band measures 2". BO loosely in patt.

Sew buttons opposite buttonholes.

Small on Texture, Big on Fit

Cable chart

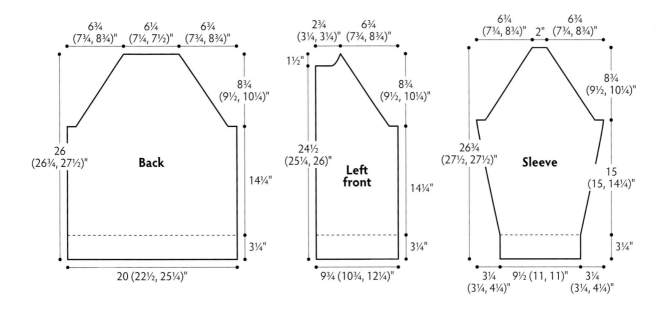

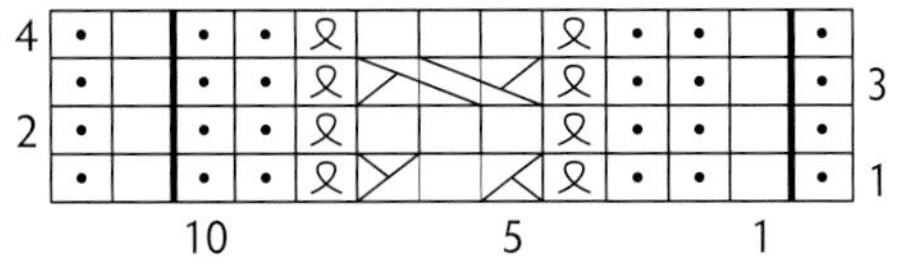

Repeat = 10 sts

☐ K on RS, P on WS

• P on RS, K on WS

K1 tbl on RS, P1 tbl on WS

Sl 2 to cn and hold in back, K1, K2 from cn

Sl 1 to cn and hold in front, K2, K1 from cn

Back

6¾ (7¾, 8¾)"   6¼ (7¼, 7½)"   6¾ (7¾, 8¾)"

8¾ (9½, 10¼)"

26 (26¾, 27½)"

14¼"

3¼"

20 (22½, 25¼)"

Left front

2¾ (3¼, 3¼)"   6¾ (7¾, 8¾)"

1½"

8¾ (9½, 10¼)"

24½ (25¼, 26)"

14¼"

3¼"

9¾ (10¾, 12¼)"

Sleeve

6¾ (7¾, 8¾)"   2"   6¾ (7¾, 8¾)"

8¾ (9½, 10¼)"

26¾ (27½, 27½)"

15 (15, 14¼)"

3¼"

3¼ (3¼, 4¼)"   9½ (11, 11)"   3¼ (3¼, 4¼)"

Waves of Winter Color

Skill level: Easy ◼◼☐☐

Size: Women's Medium (Large)

Finished bust: 37 (41)"

Finished length: 21¾ (21¾)"

MATERIALS

100% alpaca: 150 (200) g/325 (435) yds each of: (3)

A: marine heather

B: blue

C: gray heather

D: natural

Size 4 (3.5 mm) straight needles or size required to obtain gauge

Size 4 (3.5 mm) 16" circular needle for neckband

Tapestry needle

GAUGE

21 sts and 30 rows = 4" with larger needles in lace patt

PATTERN STITCHES

Lace

See chart (page 48).

Stripe pattern

Work the following sequence: *4 rows A, 2 rows D, 4 rows B, 2 rows C, 2 rows D, 2 rows A, 2 rows C, 2 rows B; rep from * throughout.

BACK

With A, CO 101 (111) sts. Beg with a WS row, knit 3 rows. Beg working lace patt and stripe sequence. Work even until piece measures 21". End after a WS row.

Shape Neck

BO center 21 (27) sts, then working each shoulder separately, BO 3 sts at each neck edge once, then BO 2 sts at each neck edge once—35 (37) sts each shoulder. When piece measures 21¾", BO rem sts.

FRONT

Work as for back until piece measures 18". End after a WS row.

Shape Neck

BO center 17 (23) sts, then working each shoulder separately, BO 3 sts each neck edge once, then BO 2 sts each neck edge once, then dec 1 st each neck edge twice—35 (37) sts each shoulder. When piece measures 21¾", BO rem sts.

SLEEVES

With A, CO 51 (61) sts. Beg with a WS row, knit 3 rows. Beg working lace patt and stripe sequence and AT THE SAME TIME, on the 3rd row and every foll 6th row inc 1 st at each end 23 times—97 (107) sts. Work even until sleeve measures 18¾". BO.

FINISHING

Weave in ends. Wash and lay flat to dry.

Sew shoulder seams. Pin center of each sleeve to body at shoulder seam and sew in sleeves. Sew side seams and underarm seams.

Neckband

With A and circular needle, RS facing, PU 96 (108) sts around neck opening, PM. Working in the round, purl 1 rnd, knit 1 rnd, BO pw.

Lace chart

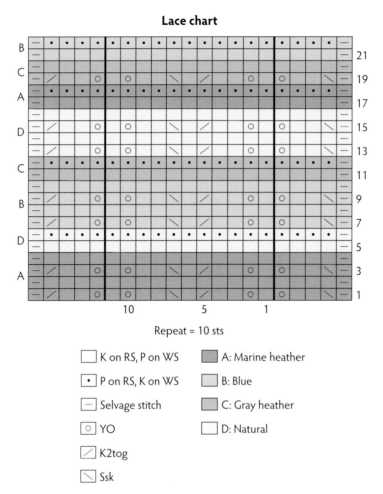

Repeat = 10 sts

☐ K on RS, P on WS	▨ A: Marine heather
• P on RS, K on WS	▨ B: Blue
— Selvage stitch	▨ C: Gray heather
○ YO	☐ D: Natural
⟋ K2tog	
⟍ Ssk	

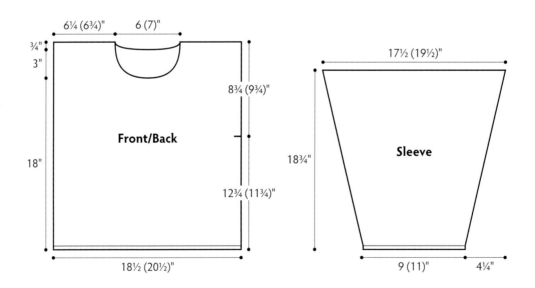

Warm and Comfy, Classic and Chic

When winter arrives, nature comes to rest, the temperature begins to fall, and we long to wrap ourselves in warm, cozy favorites. What warms body and soul better than wonderful hand-knitted vests, sweaters, and jackets? Of course, keeping warm doesn't mean you have to abandon style. The garments in this section guarantee that even in winter, you'll make a good impression.

Northern Greetings

Skill level: Intermediate ◖■■◻

Size: Women's Large/Men's Medium

Circumference: 9"

MATERIALS

Wool/nylon blend: 150 (200) g/325 (435) yds each of: **(3)**

   MC: forest green

   CC: flannel-gray heather

Set of 5 size 4 (3.5 mm) double-pointed needles or size required to obtain gauge

Tapestry needle

GAUGE

25 sts and 40 rnds = 4" in colorwork patt

22 sts and 32 rnds = 4" in St st

PATTERN STITCHES

St st in rows

RS: Knit all sts.

WS: Purl all sts.

St st in the round

Knit every rnd.

Ribbing

Multiple of 2 sts

All rnds: (K1, P1) around.

Colorwork

See chart (page 52).

Adjusting Size

The stitch repeat on these socks is too large to easily add or subtract repeats; try slightly smaller or larger needles to alter the size by changing the gauge. For example, to make an 8" circumference sock (women's Medium), use a needle size that will result in a gauge of 28 sts = 4" in the colorwork pattern.

SOCKS

Cuff

With MC, CO 48 sts. Divide sts evenly over 4 dpns and join to work in the round, being careful not to twist sts (see "Working with Double-Pointed Needles," page 110). Work in ribbing for 6¼".

Next rnd: Inc 2 sts on each needle—8 sts inc, 56 sts total.

Leg

Beg working chart A with MC and CC (see "Stranded Colorwork," page 110). After working all rows of chart A in St st, knit across the first needle with color B. Break B.

Heel Flap

Turn. With A, work heel back and forth on 28 sts (leaving other 28 sts on needles on holder or spare needle) as foll:

Next row (WS): Sl 1, K2 (edge sts), purl to last 3 sts dec 4 sts evenly across, K3 (edge sts)—24 sts rem in heel.

Next row (RS): Sl 1, knit across.

Next row: Sl 1, K2, purl to last 3 sts, K3.

Rep last 2 rows another 10 times.

Turn Heel

Working over 24 heel sts:

Next row (RS): K15, ssk, turn.

Next row (WS): P7, P2tog, turn.

Next row: Sl 1, K6, ssk, turn.

Next row: Sl 1, P6, P2tog, turn.

Rep last 2 rows until 8 sts rem in heel. End after a WS row.

Heel Gusset

With RS facing, set up sts to work in the round as foll:

Needle 1: Work across heel sts, with same needle PU 1 st in each slipped st along side of heel—11 sts PU.

Needles 2 and 3: Work across 28 held instep sts.

Needle 4: PU 1 st in each slipped st along side of heel (11 sts total), K4 to center of heel (new beg of rnd)—58 sts.

Foot

Beg working chart B in St st and AT THE SAME TIME, dec as follows until 56 sts rem:

Rnd 1: Work across needle 1 to last 3 sts, K2tog, K1, work across needles 2 and 3; on needle 4, K1, ssk, work to end of rnd.

Rnd 2: Knit.

Work even in chart B patt until foot measures 8" or approx 2½" less than desired length. Break color B.

Toe

With A, work 4 rnds even in St st.

Dec rnd 1: (K5, K2tog) around—48 sts.

Work 5 rnds even.

Dec rnd 2: (K4, K2tog) around—40 sts.

Work 4 rnds even.

Dec rnd 3: (K3, K2tog) around—32 sts.

Work 3 rnds even.

Dec rnd 4: (K2, K2tog) around—24 sts.

Work 2 rnds even.

Dec rnd 5: (K1, K2tog) around—16 sts.

Work 1 rnd even.

Dec rnd 6: K2tog around—8 sts.

FINISHING

Break yarn, run tail through rem sts.

Weave in ends. Steam or wash socks, and block on sock-blocking forms until dry.

Chart A

Repeat = 28 sts

Chart B

Repeat = 2 sts

MC: Forest green

CC: Flannel gray heather

Roses in Snow

Skill level: Easy ◼◼◻◻

Size: Women's Small (Medium, Large)

Finished bust: 39 (43, 46)"

Finished length: 22½ (22½, 23¼)"

MATERIALS

100% merino wool: 650 (700, 750) g/1145 (1230, 1320) yds, color burgundy ⑤

Size 10 (6mm) straight needles or size required to obtain gauge

Stitch markers

Tapestry needle

6 buttons, approx 1" diameter

Sewing needle and matching thread

GAUGE

16 sts and 30 rows = 4" (10 cm) in texture patt

PATTERN STITCHES

Texture

Multiple of 3+2

Row 1 (WS): *K2, (YO, sl 1 pw); rep from * to last 2 sts, K2.

Row 2: (K2, knit the next st and YO tog tbl); rep from * to last 2 sts, K2.

Rep rows 1 and 2 for patt.

NOTE

Button band, buttonhole band, and collar are worked as part of left and right fronts.

BACK

CO 82 (88, 94) sts.

Row 1 (WS): K1 (selvage), work in texture patt to last st, K1 (selvage). Cont in patt, knitting first and last st of each row for selvage sts, until piece measures 13". End after a WS row.

Shape Armholes

BO 3 sts at beg of next 2 rows, then BO 2 sts at beg of next 2 rows twice, then dec 1 st each end of row every RS row 3 times—62 (68, 74) sts rem.

Work even until piece measures 21¾ (21¾, 22½)". End after a WS row.

Shape Shoulders

BO 4 (4, 7) sts at beg of next 2 rows, then BO 5 (6, 6) sts at beg of next 2 rows 3 times. BO rem 24 sts for back neck.

LEFT FRONT

CO 44 (47, 50) sts.

Row 1 (WS): K1 (selvage), K7 (button band), PM, *K2, (YO, sl 1 pw); rep from * to last 3 sts, K2, K1 (selvage).

Row 2: K1 (selvage), (K2, knit the next st and YO tog tbl); rep from * to last 2 sts before marker, K2, slip marker, knit to end.

Rep rows 1 and 2 for patt until piece measures same as back to start of armhole shaping. End after a WS row.

Shape Armholes

BO 3 sts at beg of next RS row, then BO 2 sts at beg of next 2 RS rows twice, then dec 1 st at beg of next RS row 3 times— 34 (37, 40) sts rem.

Work even until piece measures 21¾ (21¾, 22½)". End after a WS row.

Shape Shoulders

BO 4 (4, 7) sts at beg of next RS row, then BO 5 (6, 6) sts at beg of next RS row 3 times—15 sts.

Next row: Work in patt, inc 1 st—16 sts. Work even in patt as set for 3". BO.

RIGHT FRONT

CO 44 (47, 50) sts.

Row 1 (WS): K1 (selvage), *K2, (YO, sl 1 pw); rep from * to last 10 sts, K2, PM, K7 (button band), K1 (selvage).

Row 2: K1 (selvage), K7, slip marker, (K2, knit the next st and YO tog tbl); rep from * to last 3 sts, knit to end.

Rep rows 1 and 2 for patt until piece measures same as back to start of armhole shaping. End after a RS row. AT THE SAME TIME, work buttonholes as foll:

Buttonhole rows: On row 6 and the following 26th (26th, 28th) rows (RS): K1 (selvage), K2, BO 2 sts, work rem of row in patt.

Next row: Work in patt, CO 2 sts over each gap to finish buttonhole.

Shape Armholes

BO 3 sts at beg of next WS row, then BO 2 sts at beg of next 2 WS rows twice, then dec 1 st at end of next RS row 3 times—34 (37, 40) sts rem.

Work even until piece measures 21¾ (21¾, 22½)". End after a RS row.

Shape Shoulders

BO 4 (4, 7) sts at beg of next WS row, then BO 5 (6, 6) sts at beg of next WS row 3 times—15 sts.

Next row: Work in patt, inc 1 st—16 sts. Work even in patt as set for 3". BO.

SLEEVES

CO 37 (37, 43) sts. Beg with a WS row, work in texture patt and AT THE SAME TIME, inc 1 st each end of row on 6th row and every foll 8th row 14 times—65 (65, 71) sts.

Work even until piece measures 15". End after a WS row.

Shape Cap

BO 3 sts at beg of next 2 rows, then BO 2 sts at beg of next 2 rows twice, then dec 1 st at each end of row every RS row 16 times, then BO 2 sts at beg of next 2 rows twice, then BO rem 11 (11, 17) sts.

FINISHING

Weave in ends. Wash and lay flat to dry.

Sew shoulder seams.

Pin center of each sleeve to the body at shoulder seam and sew in sleeves.

Sew side seams and underarm seams.

Neckband

Sew the two short ends of the collar together at center back. Sew bottom edge of the collar to the back neck.

Sew buttons opposite buttonholes.

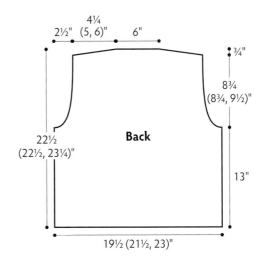

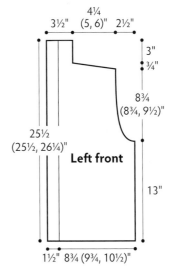

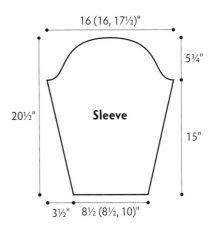

Modern Icelandic Sweater

Skill level: Experienced ◼◼◼▶

Size: Women's Medium/Large

Finished bust: 43"

Finished length: 25¼"

MATERIALS

100% alpaca: (3)

    A: 650 g/1420 yds, color gray

    B: 100 g/220 yds, color natural

    C: 100 g/220 yds, color burgundy heather

Several size 6 (4 mm) circular needles, ranging from 16" to 48" long, or size required to obtain gauge

Size 4 (3.5 mm) 29" circular needle and set of 5 double-pointed needles

Contrasting scrap yarn for provisional CO

Size E-4 (3.5 mm) crochet hook for provisional CO

Stitch markers

Stitch holders

Tapestry needle

GAUGE

24 sts and 32 rnds = 4" with larger needles in St st

24 sts and 26 rnds = 4" with larger needles in colorwork patt

PATTERN STITCHES

St st in rows

RS: Knit all sts.

WS: Purl all sts.

St st in the round

Knit every rnd.

Ribbing

Multiple of 4 sts

All rnds: (K2, P2) around.

Colorwork

See charts A and B (pages 58 and 59).

NOTE ABOUT CAST ONS

Pieces are cast on using the tubular method. Approximately half of the sts are cast on provisionally, then increased to the total amount in the first row. When scrap yarn is removed, the hem will have a smooth edge that curves around to the WS.

BODY

The front and back are worked tog in the round; the beg of the round is the right side "seam."

With scrap yarn and smaller circular needle, CO 130 sts using a provisional method (see "Provisional Cast On," page 107), PM and join to work in the round, being careful not to twist sts.

Change to A and inc to 260 sts as foll:

Rnd 1: (K1, YO) around.

Rnds 2 and 4: (Sl 1 pw wyib, P1).

Rnd 3: (K1, sl 1 pw wyif).

Rnd 5: (K1, sl 1 to cn and hold in back, K1, P1 from cn, P1).

Work in ribbing for 2¾".

Next rnd: Change to larger needles and St st, work all rnds of chart A (see "Stranded Colorwork," page 110), then cont with color A and work even until piece measures 12¼" from top of ribbing.

Divide for Front and Back

K122, BO 8 sts, K122, BO 8 sts.

Shape Armholes

For back, over the following 122 sts, *work back and forth in St st and BO 2 sts at beg of next 2 rows twice, then dec 1 st at each end of row every RS row twice—110 sts rem.

When piece measures 16¼", place sts on hold and rep from * for front on rem 122 sts.

SLEEVES

Sleeves are worked in the round from cuff to shoulder.

With dpns and scrap yarn, CO 30 sts as for body, PM and join for working in the round, being careful not to twist sts.

Change to color A and inc to 60 sts as for body, then work in ribbing as for 2¾".

Change to shortest larger circular needle and knit 2 rnds, then work chart A, then cont in St st with color A and AT THE SAME TIME, inc as foll, changing to longer circular needles as needed:

Every 4th rnd, inc 1 st at beg and end of rnd 20 times, then inc 1 st at beg and end of rnd every other rnd 11 times—122 sts.

When piece measures 14" from top of ribbing, beg working back and forth in St st and BO 4 sts at beg of next 2 rows once, then BO 2 sts at beg of next 2 rows twice, then dec 1 st each end of every RS row twice—102 sts rem.

When sleeve measures 18", place all sts on hold.

YOKE

Place sts on longest larger circular needle as foll, 110 sts of back, PM, then 102 sts of one sleeve, PM, then 110 sts of front, PM, then 102 sts of second sleeve, PM—424 sts total. ***Note:*** As yoke progresses, change to progressively shorter circular needles.

Rnd 1: Knit to last st of back, K2tog, knit to last st of sleeve, K2tog, knit to last st of front, K2tog, knit to last st of second sleeve, K2tog—420 sts rem. Remove all markers except that at end of rnd.

Rnd 2: Dec 40 sts evenly around—380 sts.

Work chart B in St st, dec as shown in chart—152 sts rem. With A, work 2 rnds in St st, then dec 32 sts evenly on next rnd—120 sts.

BO. Piece measures approx 25¼".

FINISHING

Weave in ends. Wash and lay flat to dry.

Sew underarm seams.

With smaller circular needle and A, RS facing, PU 120 sts around neck, PM. Working in the round, work in ribbing for 8". BO loosely in patt.

Chart A

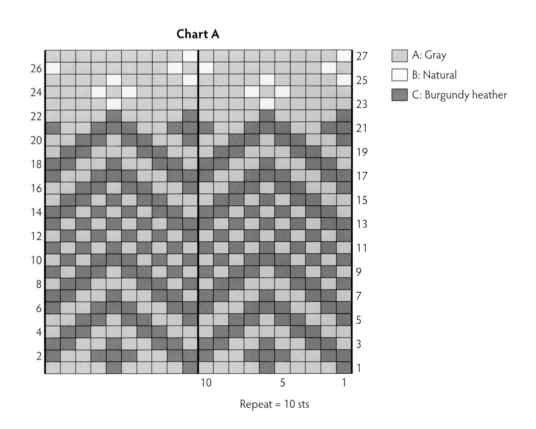

	A: Gray
	B: Natural
	C: Burgundy heather

Repeat = 10 sts

Chart B

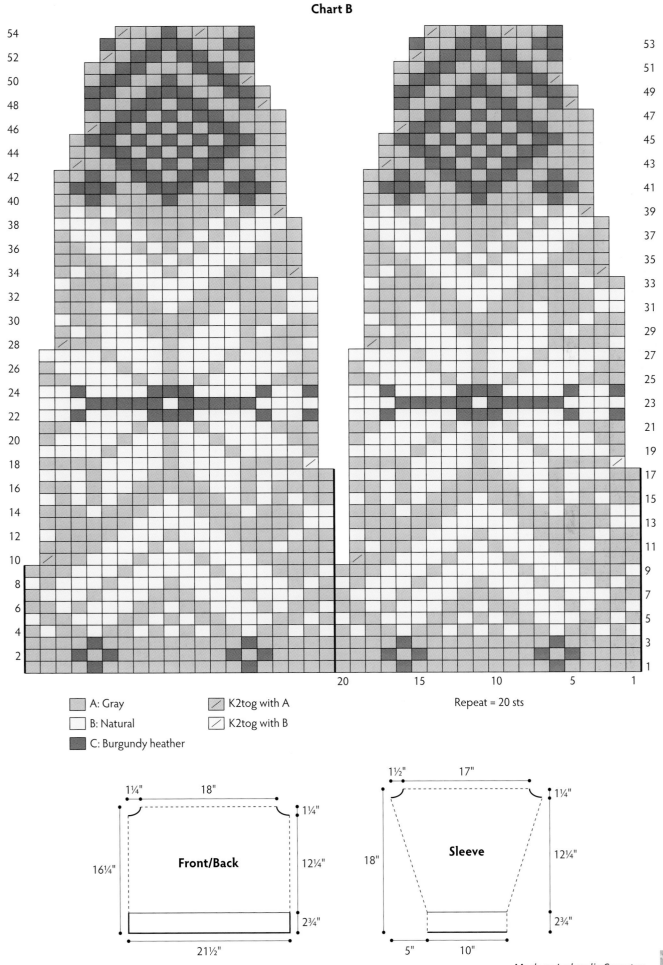

▨ A: Gray	◪ K2tog with A	
☐ B: Natural	◨ K2tog with B	
▦ C: Burgundy heather		

Repeat = 20 sts

Front/Back

Sleeve

Timeless Elegance

Skill level: Intermediate ◼◼◼◻

Size: Women's Medium/Large

Finished bust: 46½"

Finished length: 34¾"

Scarf: 11" x 79"

MATERIALS FOR JACKET

100% merino wool 🄵

   MC: 850 g/1495 yds, color dark gray heather

   CC: 400 g/705 yds, color beige heather

Size 8 (5 mm) and 10 (6 mm) straight needles or size required to obtain gauge

Size 8 (5 mm) and 10 (6 mm) 47" circular needles for bands

Stitch markers

Tapestry needle

8 buttons, approx 1¼" diameter

Sewing needle and matching thread

MATERIALS FOR SCARF

100% merino wool: 400 g/705 yds, color dark gray heather 🄵

Size 8 (5 mm) straight needles or size required to obtain gauge

Tapestry needle

GAUGE

17 sts and 20 rows = 4" with larger needles in colorwork patt

21 sts and 24 rows = 4" with smaller needles in ribbing patt

PATTERN STITCHES

Ribbing

Multiple of 6+3 sts

Row 1 (RS): K3, (P3, K3) across.

Row 2: Work sts as they appear.

Rep rows 1 and 2 for patt.

Colorwork

See chart (page 63).

St st

RS: Knit all sts.

WS: Purl all sts.

Rev St st

RS: Purl all sts.

WS: Knit all sts.

Jacket

Back and front are worked together in one piece to armholes.

BODY

With smaller needles and MC, CO 173 sts.

Row 1 (WS): Knit.

Work 4 rows in rev St st.

Change to larger needles and set up charted color patt in St st as foll (see "Stranded Colorwork," page 110):

Row 1 (RS): K1 (selvage), work first 2 sts of chart, PM, rep 24-st chart rep 7 times across, PM, work the last st of chart, K1 (selvage). Cont in patt, knitting first and last st of each row for selvage sts until piece measures 25¼". End after a WS row.

Divide for Front and Back

Next row (RS): Work 29 sts (right front) in patt as est, BO 17 sts, work 81 sts as est (back), BO 17 sts, work rem 29 sts in patt as est (left front).

Left Front

Working over the 29 left front sts, work even until piece measures 34". End after a WS row.

Shape shoulder: BO 9 sts at beg of next RS row, then BO 10 sts at beg of next RS row twice—all sts consumed.

Back

Working over the 81 back sts, work even until piece measures 34". End after a WS row.

Shape shoulders and neck: BO 9 sts at beg of next 2 rows, then BO 10 sts at beg of next 2 rows twice. AT THE SAME TIME, after the first shoulder BO, BO center 15 sts for the neck, then working each shoulder separately, BO 4 sts at each neck edge once—all sts consumed.

Right Front

Working over the 29 right front sts, work even until piece measures 34". End after a RS row.

Shape shoulder: BO 9 sts at beg of next WS row, then BO 10 sts at beg of next WS row twice—all sts consumed.

SLEEVES

With smaller needles and MC, CO 56 sts and work in ribbing for 9¾". On the last row (WS), inc 5 sts evenly across—61 sts. Change to larger needles. Set up color patt as foll:

Set up row (RS): K1 (selvage), work sts 19–24 of chart once, rep sts 1–24 of chart twice across, work sts 1–5 of chart once, K1 (selvage). Cont in patt, knitting first

and last st of each row for selvage, and AT THE SAME TIME, inc 1 st at beg and end of rnd every 6th rnd twice, then every 4th rnd 6 times, working sts into colorwork patt—77 sts. Work even until sleeve measures 19¾", BO all sts.

FINISHING

Weave in ends. Wash and lay flat to dry.

Button Band

With smaller circular needle and MC, RS facing, PU 167 sts along the lower 31½" of the left front edge. Work in ribbing for 7", knitting first and last st each row for selvage sts. BO loosely in patt.

Buttonhole Band

With smaller circular needle and MC, RS facing, PU 167 sts along the lower 31½" of the right front edge and work in ribbing as for the left front and AT THE SAME TIME, work buttonholes as foll.

Work even until ribbing measures 2¼". End after a WS row.

Next (buttonhole) row (RS): Work 118 sts in ribbing, * BO 3 sts, work 9 sts in ribbing; rep from * twice, BO 3 sts, work in ribbing to end of row—4 buttonholes.

Next row (WS): Work in ribbing as est, CO 3 sts over each gap to finish buttonholes.

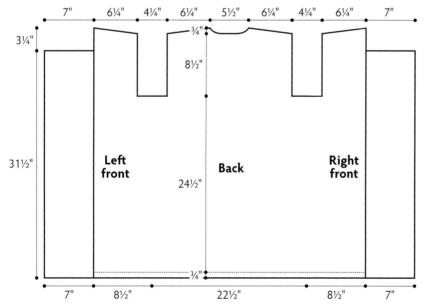

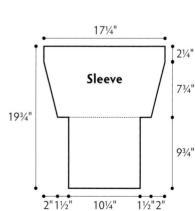

Work another 2¾" of ribbing and rep buttonholes.

When band measures 7", BO loosely in patt.

Collar

Working around the upper 3¼" of the front edges (above the bands) and across the back neck, with smaller circular needle and MC, RS facing, PU 83 sts. Work in ribbing for 4", knitting first and last st each row for selvage sts. Change to larger circular needle and work in patt for 3" more. BO loosely in patt.

Scarf

With small needles and MC, CO 59 sts and beg and ending with a WS row, work in ribbing for 79", knitting first and last st each row for selvage sts. BO loosely in patt.

FINISHING

Weave in ends.

Colorwork chart

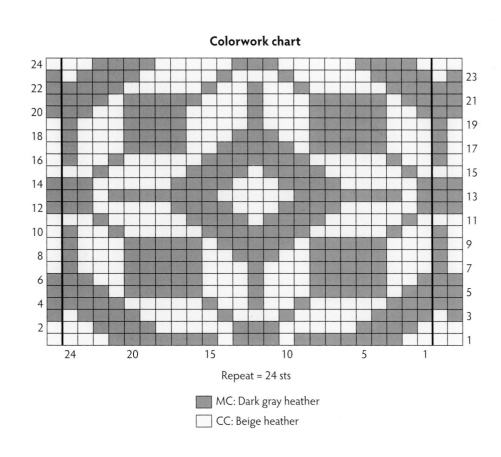

Repeat = 24 sts

MC: Dark gray heather
CC: Beige heather

A Winter's Tale

Skill level: Experienced ■■■▶

Size: Women's Small (Medium, Large)

Finished bust: 39 (43, 46)"

Finished length: 29¼ (29¼, 29¼)"

MATERIALS

100% merino wool: 1100 (1150, 1200) g/1935 (2025, 2110) yds, color medium gray heather ⑤

Size 10 (6 mm) straight needles or size required to obtain gauge

Size 8 (5 mm) 47" circular needle and set of 5 double-pointed needles for bands and belt

Stitch markers

Cable needle

Tapestry needle

5 buttons, approx 1½" diameter

Sewing needle and matching thread

Cardboard for pompoms

GAUGE

23 sts and 24 rows = 4" with larger needles in cables and ribbing patt

PATTERN STITCHES

Ribbing

Multiple of 4+2 sts

Row 1 (RS): K2, (P2, K2) across.

Row 2: Work sts as they appear.

Rep rows 1 and 2 for patt.

Cable

See chart (page 67). **Note:** Work sts on WS rows as they appear.

BACK

Using the long tail CO (page 106) and larger needles, CO 114 (122, 130) sts. Work in rib as foll:

Setup Row: K1 (selvage), P1, (K2, P2) to last 4 sts, K2, P1, K1 (selvage).

Work in ribbing as est until piece measures 5". Set up cable patt as foll:

Row 1 (RS): K1 (selvage), work 13 (17, 21) sts in ribbing as est, PM, work cable patt over next 30 sts, PM, work 26 sts in ribbing as est, PM, work cable patt over next 30 sts, PM, work in ribbing as est over next 13 (17, 21) sts, K1 (selvage).

Work in patt as est, knitting first and last st of each row for selvage sts until piece measures 20 (19½, 18¾)". End after a WS row.

Raglan Shaping

BO 4 sts at beg of next 2 rows for armholes—106 (114, 122) sts. Dec 2 sts each end of row every RS row 0 (2, 4) times then every 4th row 13 times as foll:

Dec row (RS): K1 (selvage), K1, sl 1, K2tog, psso, work in patt to last 4 sts, K3tog, K1, K1 (selvage)—54 sts. Work even in patt until piece measures 29¼". BO rem sts, AT THE SAME TIME, work P2tog over each purl section in center 30 sts.

LEFT FRONT

Using the long tail CO and larger needles (see "Long Tail Cast On," page 106), CO 58 (62, 66) sts. Work in ribbing as for back. When piece measures same as back to beg of cable patt, set up patt as foll:

Row 1 (RS): K1 (selvage), work 13 (15, 17) sts in ribbing as est, PM, work cable patt over next 30 sts, PM, work in ribbing over next 13 (15, 17) sts, K1 (selvage). Work even until piece measures 18¾". End with a WS row.

Neck Shaping

Next (dec) row (RS): Work in patt to 5 sts before end, K3tog, work in patt to end.

Next row: Work even in patt.

Rep last 2 rows 5 times—46 (50, 54) sts. Cont in patt, rep dec row every 4th row 7 times.

Raglan Shaping

AT THE SAME TIME, when piece measures 20 (19½, 18¾)", shape armhole edge as foll (cont working neck shaping as set):

BO 4 sts at beg of next RS row for armhole. Dec 2 sts at beg of row every RS row 0 (2, 4) times then every 4th row 12 times as foll:

Dec row (RS): K1 (selvage), K1, sl 1, K2tog, psso, work in patt to end—4 sts. Work even in patt until piece measures 28½". BO.

RIGHT FRONT

Work as for left front to start of neck shaping. End with a WS row.

Neck Shaping

Next (dec) row (RS): K1 (selvage), K1, sl 1, K2tog, psso, work in patt to end.

Next row: Work even in patt.

Rep last 2 rows 5 times—46 (50, 54) sts. Cont in patt, rep dec row every 4th row 7 times.

RAGLAN SHAPING

AT THE SAME TIME, when piece measures 20 (19½, 18¾)", shape armhole edge as foll (cont working neck shaping as set):

BO 4 sts at beg of next WS row for armhole. Dec 2 sts at end of row every RS row 0 (2, 4) times then every 4th row 12 times as foll:

Dec row (RS): Work in patt to 5 sts before end, K3tog, work in patt to end. Finish as for left front.

LEFT SLEEVE

Using the long tail CO and larger needles (see "Long Tail Cast On," page 106), CO 58 (58, 66) sts and work in ribbing as for back. When piece measures 5", PM before and after center 30 sts on the sleeve and beg working cable patt between markers, while continuing to work in ribbing as est on rem sts.

AT THE SAME TIME, every 4th row, inc 1 st each end of row once, then inc 1 st each end of row every 12th (8th, 8th) row 7 (11, 11) times—74 (82, 90) sts.

Raglan Shaping

When piece measures 15¾", BO 4 sts at beg of next 2 rows—66 (74, 82) sts.

On the right edge (beg of RS rows), shape as for back, dec 2 sts each end of row every RS row 0 (2, 4) times, then every 4th row 13 times. On the left edge (end of RS rows), shape as for left front, dec 2 sts at beg of row every RS row 0 (2, 4) times, then every 4th row 12 times—16 sts. At beg of WS rows, BO 6 sts once, then BO 5 sts twice.

RIGHT SLEEVE

Work as for left sleeve to start of raglan shaping.

Raglan Shaping

When piece measures 15¾", BO 4 sts at beg of next 2 rows—66 (74, 82) sts.

On the left edge (end of RS rows), shape as for back, dec 2 sts each end of row every RS row 0 (2, 4) times, then every 4th row 13 times. On the right edge (beg of RS rows), shape as for left front, dec 2 sts at beg of row every RS row 0 (2, 4) times, then every 4th row 12 times—16 sts. At beg of RS rows, BO 6 sts once, then BO 5 sts twice.

BELT

With dpns, CO 20 sts. Join to work in the round, being careful not to twist sts. Work in St st until belt measures 60", BO with a double strand of yarn. Make 2 pompoms 2" in diameter (see "Pompoms," page 110) and attach 1 to each end of belt.

FINISHING

Weave in ends. Wash pieces and lay flat to dry. Sew the raglan, sleeve, and side seams.

Front Bands/Collar

The collar portion of the ribbed bands is shaped by working short rows.

With circular needle, RS facing, PU 105 sts along the right front to the beg of neck shaping, then PU 96 sts to center back of neck, PM, PU 96 sts to the neck shaping on left front, then PU 105 sts down left front to bottom edge—402 sts.

Row 1 (WS): P2, work in ribbing to marker at center back of neck, work 31 sts past the marker, wrap and turn.

Row 2 (RS): Sl 1, then work 62 sts, wrap and turn.

Row 3: Sl 1, work in ribbing to 8 sts past wrap at opposite end (pick up wrap and work tog with st), wrap and turn.

Row 4: Rep row 3.

Work rows 3 and 4 another 14 times—190 sts worked in short rows. Next row, work in ribbing across all sts.

AT THE SAME TIME, when band measures 1", work buttonholes on right front as foll:

Next (buttonhole) row (RS): Work 6 sts in patt, BO 2 sts, *work 22 sts in patt, BO 2 sts; rep from * 3 times, work in patt to end—5 buttonholes.

Next row, work in ribbing as est, CO 2 sts over each gap to finish buttonholes. Work even in ribbing until bands measure approx 2¾". BO loosely in patt.

Pompoms

Make 17 pompoms approx 1" in diameter (see "Pompoms," page 110). Sew 3 pompoms to each sleeve cuff and sew the remaining 11 pompoms to the front band using the photo as a guide for placement.

Cable chart

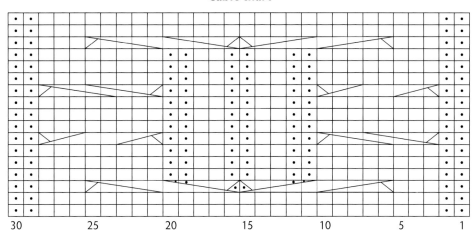

Cable pattern = 30 sts

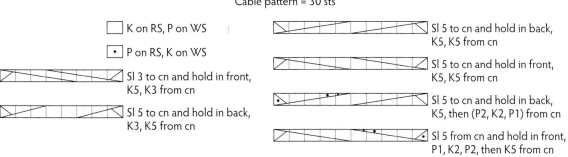

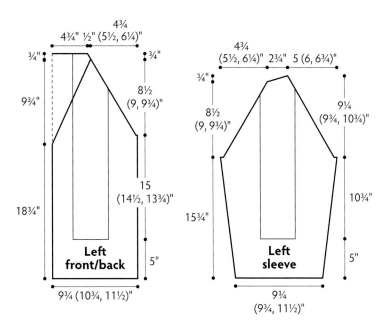

Cables on Cables

Skill level: Experienced ◼◼◼▶

Size: Women's Small (Medium, Large)

Finished bust: 35¼ (38¼, 41¼)"

Finished length: 19¾ (20½, 21¼)"

MATERIALS

100% merino wool: 500 (550, 600) g/1380 (1520, 1655) yds, color beige heather ③

Size 4 (3.5 mm) and 6 (4 mm) straight needles or size required to obtain gauge

Size 4 (3.5 mm) 47" circular needle for bands

Stitch markers

Stitch holders

Cable needle

Tapestry needle

4 (4, 5) buttons, approx 1" diameter

Sewing needle and matching thread

GAUGE

22 sts and 32 rows = 4" with larger needles in St st

30 sts and 32 rows = 4" with larger needles in cable patt

PATTERN STITCHES

Rev St st

RS: Purl all sts.

WS: Knit all sts.

Ribbing

Multiple of 4 sts

Row 1 (RS): (K2, P2) across.

Row 2: Work sts as they appear.

Rep rows 1 and 2 for patt.

Cable

See chart (page 71). **Note:** Work sts on WS rows as they appear.

Selvage Stitches

On this vest, 2 selvage stitches were worked at the beginning and end of each row. The first stitch is knit through the back loop and the second stitch is worked in St st (knit on RS, purled on WS). At the end of the row, the second to last stitch is worked in St st (knit on RS, purled on WS), and the last stitch is slipped purlwise.

BACK

With smaller needles, CO 144 (152, 168) sts and work in ribbing between the selvage sts as foll:

Row 1 (WS): K1 tbl, P1 (selvage), PM, K1, (P2, K2) to last 5 sts, P2, K1, PM, P1, sl 1 pw wyif.

Row 2: K1 tbl, K1 (selvage), slip marker, work ribbing sts as they appear to next marker, slip marker, K1, sl 1 pw wyib.

Work in patt as est until piece measures 2". On the last row (WS), inc 2 (4, 2) sts—146 (156, 170) sts.

Change to larger needles and set up cable patt as foll:

Next row (RS): Work 8 (13, 8) sts in rev St st with 2 selvage sts, PM, work cable patt over next 130 (130, 154) sts as foll, PM, work to end of row in rev St st and 2 selvage sts as set.

For sizes Small and Medium: Work the 62-st rep twice, then the last 6 sts of chart.

For size Large: Work sts 1–12 once, work 62-st rep once, work sts 1–68 once, then end with sts 57–68.

Work in patt as est until piece measures 9¾" above ribbing. End after a WS row.

Shape Armholes and Shoulders

BO 13 sts at beg of next 2 rows—120 (130, 144) sts rem.

When piece measures 17¾ (18½, 19¼)" from top of band, put center 74 sts on hold for hood and BO rem 23 (28, 35) sts in each shoulder.

LEFT FRONT

With smaller needles, CO 63 (67, 75) sts and work in ribbing as foll:

Row 1 (WS): K1 tbl, P1 (selvage), PM, (P2, K2) to last 5 sts, P2, K1, PM, P1, sl 1 pw wyif.

Row 2: K1 tbl, K1 (selvage), slip marker, work ribbing sts as they appear to next marker, slip marker, K1, sl 1 pw wyib.

When ribbing measures 2", on last row (WS) inc 3 (4, 3) sts—66 (71, 78) sts.

Change to larger needles and set up cable patt as foll:

Next row (RS): Work the first 8 (13, 8) sts in rev St st with 2 selvage sts, PM, work cable patt over the next 56 (56, 68) sts as foll, then end with the 2 selvage sts as est.

For sizes Small and Medium: Work sts 1–56 of chart.

For size Large: Work sts 1–12 once, then sts 1–56.

Work even until piece measures same as back to armhole.

Shape Armhole and Shoulder

BO 13 sts at beg of next RS row—53 (58, 65) sts. Work even until piece measures same as back to shoulder. Place last 30 sts (neck edge) on hold, BO rem 23 (28, 35) shoulder sts.

RIGHT FRONT

Work as for left front to start of cable patt.

Change to larger needles and set up cable patt as foll:

Next row (RS): Work 2 selvage sts, work cable patt over next 56 (56, 68) sts as foll, PM, work last 8 (13, 8) sts in rev St st with 2 selvage sts.

For sizes Small and Medium: Work sts 1–56 of chart.

For size Large: Work sts 1–12 once, then sts 1–56.

Work even until piece measures same as back to armhole.

Shape Armhole and Shoulder

BO 13 sts at beg of next WS row—53 (58, 65) sts. Work even until piece measures same as back to shoulder. Place first 30 sts (neck edge) on hold, BO rem 23 (28, 35) shoulder sts.

FINISHING

Weave in ends. Wash piece and lay flat to dry. Sew shoulder seams.

Hood

With RS facing, place the 30 right front sts, 74 back sts, and 30 left front sts on needles. On the first row (WS), inc 38 sts evenly over the back 74 sts—172 sts.

Next row (RS): Work 2 selvage sts, work sts 13–62 of cable chart once, then the 62 sts rep once, then sts 1–56 once, then end with the 2 selvage sts.

When hood measures 12¼", BO and sew top seam.

Armbands

With RS facing, PU 104 (112, 120) sts around armhole. Work in ribbing as for back for 2".

Next row (RS): Dec 1 st on each end so there is only 1 selvage st at each end of row.

Next row (WS): Work even in patt. BO loosely in patt.

Sew side seams, including edges of bands.

Front Bands

With circular needle, RS facing, PU 136 (142, 148) sts along front edge of vest, 140 sts across front edge of hood, and 136 (142, 148) sts along second edge of vest—412 (424, 436) sts. Work in ribbing as for armbands. AT THE SAME TIME, when band measures 1", make 4 (4, 5) buttonholes on right front as foll:

Next (buttonhole) row (RS): Work 2 selvage sts, work 9 (13, 5) sts as est, *ssk, YO, K2tog, work 32 (32, 28) sts in patt; rep from * 2 (2, 3) times, ssk, YO, K2tog, work to end of row in patt as est.

Next row: Work in ribbing as est, knitting into the front and back of each YO. When band measures 2", work last 2 rows as for armholes. BO loosely in patt. Weave in ends.

Sew buttons opposite buttonholes.

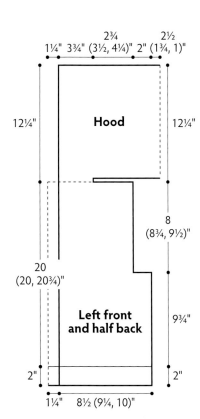

Hood

12¼"

2¾
1¼" 3¾" (3½, 4¼)" 2" (1¾, 1)"
2½

12¼"

8
(8¾, 9½)"

20
(20, 20¾)"

Left front and half back

9¾"

2"

2"

1¼"   8½ (9¼, 10)"

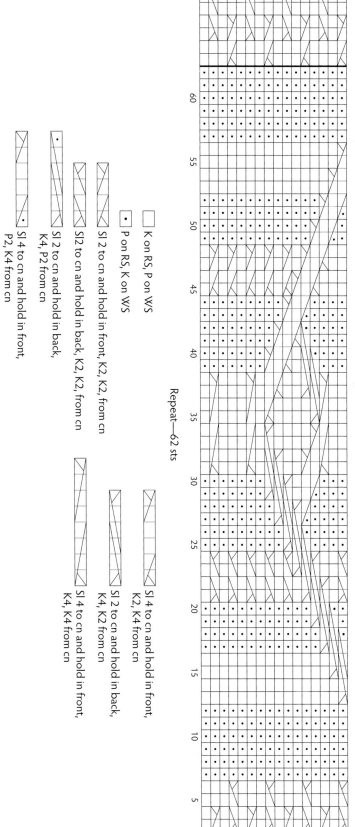

Cable chart

Repeat—62 sts

☐ K on RS, P on WS

• P on RS, K on WS

⬚ Sl 4 to cn and hold in front,
P2, K4 from cn

⬚ Sl 2 to cn and hold in back,
K4, P2 from cn

⬚ Sl 2 to cn and hold in back, K2, K2, from cn

⬚ Sl 2 to cn and hold in front, K2, K2, K2, from cn

⬚ Sl 4 to cn and hold in front,
K4, K4 from cn

⬚ Sl 2 to cn and hold in back,
K4, K2 from cn

⬚ Sl 4 to cn and hold in front,
K2, K4 from cn

Messenger Bag

Skill level: Intermediate ◼◼◼▢

Size: One size

Finished measurements: 14" x 16¾"

MATERIALS

Wool/acrylic blend: 200 g/410 yds each of:

   MC: gray heather

   CC: white marble

Size 7 (4.5 mm) 32" circular needle or size required to obtain gauge

Stitch markers

Tapestry needle

GAUGE

21 sts and 25 rows = 4" (10 cm) in colorwork patt

PATTERN STITCHES

St st

RS: Knit all sts.

WS: Purl all sts.

Ribbing

Multiple of 4 sts

All rnds: (K2, P2) around.

Colorwork

See chart at right.

BAG

With MC, CO 176 sts. PM and join for working in the rnd. Work in chart A in St st for 4". With MC, work in garter st for 4 rnds. Change to chart B and work all rnds of chart twice, then work rnd 1 once more. With MC, work in garter st for 4 rnds. Change to chart A and work even until piece measures 13¾". Change to MC and work in ribbing for 2½". BO loosely in patt.

STRAPS

Make 2 alike.

With MC, CO 8 sts. Work in I-cord as foll:

Row 1: Work row 1 of chart A. At end of row, do not turn, slide sts to opposite end of needle to work next row. Cont as set until piece measures 25½". BO.

FINISHING

Weave in ends. Wash, block pieces to measurements, and dry flat. Sew bottom seam. Fold the ribbing to outside and tack in place. On the inside of bag, sew straps in place overlapping edge by 1½".

Chart A

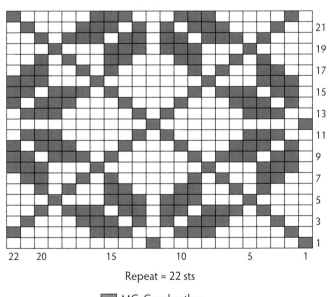

Repeat = 2 sts

Chart B

Repeat = 22 sts

◼ MC: Gray heather

☐ CC: White marble

Classic Ribbed Raglan

Skill level: Intermediate ●●●▢

Size: Women's Small (Medium, Large)

Finished bust: 36 (39, 43)"

Finished length: 25 (25, 25)"

MATERIALS

100% merino wool: 350 (350, 400) g/965 (965, 1095) yds, color violet 〔3〕

Size 4 (3.5 mm) straight needles or size required to obtain gauge

Size 4 (3.5 mm) 16" circular needle for neckband

Tapestry needle

GAUGE

23 sts and 38 rows = 4" (10 cm) with larger needles in brioche ribbing patt

PATTERN STITCHES

Brioche ribbing in rows

Multiple of 4 sts

Row 1 (WS): *K1, P1, (YO, sl 1 pw), K1; rep from * across.

Row 2 (RS): *P1, knit the next st and YO tog, (YO, sl 1 pw), P1; rep from * across.

Row 3: *K1, purl the next st and YO tog, (YO, sl 1 pw), K1; rep from * across.

Rep rows 2 and 3 for patt.

Brioche ribbing in the round

Multiple of 4 sts

Rnd 1: *K1, (YO, sl 1 pw), K1, P1; rep from * around.

Rnd 2: *P1, knit the next st and YO tog, (YO, sl 1 pw), P1; rep from * around.

Rnd 3: *P1, (YO, sl 1 pw), knit the next st and YO tog, P1; rep from * around.

Rep rnds 2 and 3 for patt.

BACK

With the long tail cast on (see "Long Tail Cast On," page 106), CO 106, 114, 122 sts.

Row 1 (WS): K1 (selvage), work in brioche ribbing in rows to last st, K1 (selvage). Work even in patt, knitting first and last st of each row for selvage sts until piece measures 17 (16¼, 15½)". End after a WS row.

Raglan Shaping

For armhole, BO 4 sts at beg of next 2 rows—98 (106, 114) sts.

Dec 1 st at each end of row every RS row 38 (42, 46) times as foll:

Dec row (RS): K1 (selvage), K3, P2tog, work in patt until 6 sts before end of row, P2tog, K3, K1 (selvage)—22 sts. Work even in patt until piece measures 25". BO.

FRONT

Work as for back, rep dec row 33 (37, 41) times—32 sts.

Neck Shaping

When 32 sts rem (piece measures approx 23½"), BO center 12 sts for the neck, then working each side separately, every other row dec 3 sts each neck edge once, then dec 2 sts each neck edge twice—3 sts. BO.

LEFT SLEEVE

With long tail cast on, CO 50 (58, 58) sts and beg working in brioche rib patt as for back and AT THE SAME TIME, shape sleeve as foll, working all new sts into brioche rib:

For sizes Small and Medium: Every 8th row, inc 1 st each end of row 3 times, then inc 1 st each end of row every 6th row 21 times—98 (106) sts.

For size Large: Every 6th row, inc 1 st each end of row 19 times, then inc 1 st each end of row every 4th row 9 times—114 sts.

Work even until sleeve measures 15¾". End after a WS row.

Raglan Shaping

BO 4 sts at beg of next 2 rows—90 (98, 106) sts.

Work raglan shaping as for back, dec 1 st at beg of RS rows 38 (42, 46) times and dec 1 st at end of RS rows 33 (37, 41) times, and AT THE SAME TIME, shape top of cap as foll:

After the 33 (37, 41) raglan dec on ends of RS rows have been completed, at beg of next WS row BO 7 sts, then every WS row BO 3 sts at neck edge 4 times, while continuing to work raglan dec at beg of RS rows—all sts are consumed.

RIGHT SLEEVE

Work as for left sleeve to beg of raglan shaping.

Raglan Shaping

BO 4 sts at beg of next 2 rows—90 (98, 106) sts.

Work raglan shaping as for back, dec 1 st at end of RS rows 38 (42, 46) times and dec 1 st at beg of RS rows 33 (37, 41) times, and AT THE SAME TIME, shape top of cap as foll:

After the 33 (37, 41) raglan dec on beg of RS rows have been completed, at beg of next RS row BO 7 sts, then every RS row BO 3 sts at neck edge 4 times, while continuing to work raglan dec at end of RS rows—all sts are consumed.

FINISHING

Weave in ends. Sew raglan seams, underarm, and side seams.

Collar

With circular needle and WS facing you, PU 88 sts around neck opening and work in brioche rib in the round until collar measures 8". BO. Fold collar in half to outside.

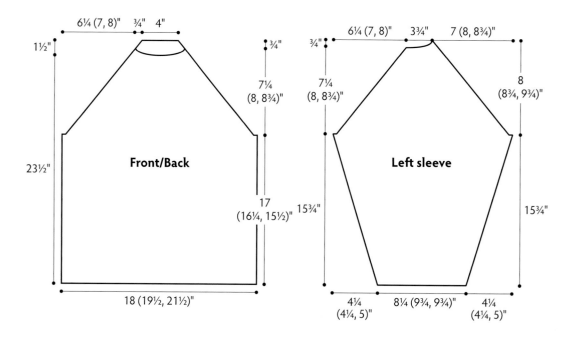

Well-Dressed to Brave the Cold

Not only are refined accessories like caps, shawls, and ponchos a practical source of warmth, but they also add that certain something to just about any outfit. Whether you're planning a trip to the mall for holiday shopping, enjoying an evening of hot mulled wine with friends, or spending an early morning shoveling the freshly fallen snow, the garments and accessories in this section will let you give winter weather the cold shoulder in style.

Romantic Frills

Skill level: Intermediate ◾◾◾◻

Size: One size

Finished circumference:

   Poncho: 43"

   Hat: Approx 22"

MATERIALS

100% alpaca: 100 g/220 yds each of: (3)

   MC: black

   CC: light gray

Size 7 (4.5 mm) 30" and 47" circular needles and set of 5 double-pointed needles, or size required to obtain gauge

Size 7 (4.5 mm) crochet hook

Stitch markers

Tapestry needle

GAUGE

22 sts and 23 rows = 4" in St st

32 rnds of colorwork = 4¾"

25 rnds of ribbing = 4"

PATTERN STITCHES

St st in the round

Knit every rnd.

Ribbing (for poncho)

Multiple of 5 sts

All rnds: (K3, P2) around.

Ribbing (for hat)

Multiple of 4 sts

All rnds: (K2, P2) around.

Colorwork

See chart (page 80).

Poncho

With MC and shorter circular needle, CO 240 sts. PM and join to work in the round, being careful not to twist sts. Work in ribbing for 23½", then work in St st for 6¼", then work all rows of chart in St st (see "Stranded Colorwork," page 110). Knit 1 rnd in MC.

RUFFLE

Rnd 1: (PM, K1, PM, P5) around.

Next (inc) rnd: *Slip marker, M1, K1, M1, slip marker, P5; rep from * around—320 sts.

Next rnd: Work even, knitting M1 sts.

Next rnd: *Slip marker, M1, knit to marker, M1, slip marker, P5; rep from * around.

Rep last 2 sts until there are 9 knit sts between each pair of markers—560 sts. Work even until ruffle measures 3½". BO loosely in patt.

FINISHING

Weave in ends. Wash and lay flat to dry.

Cut rem MC yarn into 10" lengths and group 2 or 3 strands tog for each strand of fringe (see "Fringe," page 110). With crochet hook, attach fringe in each purl section around CO edge.

Hat

With MC and dpns, CO 84 sts. Join to work in the round, being careful not to twist sts. Work in ribbing for ¾", knit 2 rnds, then work all rows of chart in St st. Do not cut CC.

Next rnd: With MC, (K3, P3) around.

Next 2 rnds: (With CC K3, with MC P3) around.

Cut CC.

Next rnd: With MC, (K3, P3) around.

Next rnd: (K2tog, K1, P3) around—70 sts.

Next rnd: (K2tog, P3) around—56 sts.

RUFFLE

Work as for poncho until there are 9 knit sts between each pair of markers—168 sts. Work even until ruffle measures 3½". BO loosely in patt.

FINISHING

Weave in ends. Wash and lay flat to dry.

Weave a strand of yarn in and out below the ruffle and gather in the top of the hat. Bring yarn ends to inside, tie to fasten off.

Colorwork chart

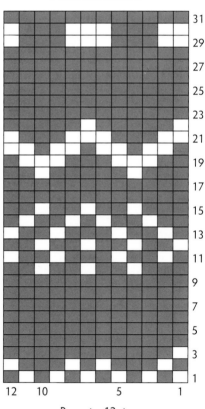

Repeat = 12 sts

■ MC: Black
□ CC: Light gray

Vintage French

Skill level: Intermediate ◼◼◼◻

Size: One size

Finished measurements:

Scarf: 14" x 75"

Hat: Approx 22" circumference

MATERIALS

100% wool: 850 g/1480 yds, color natural silver ⑤

Size 10 (6 mm) straight needles and set of 5 double-
pointed needles or size required to obtain gauge

Stitch markers

Cable needle

Size H-8 (5 mm) crochet hook

Tapestry needle

Cardboard for pompoms

GAUGE

13 sts and 22 rows = 4" (10 cm) in seed st

36 sts = 6¼" in chart A patt

14 sts = 3¼" in chart B patt

PATTERN STITCHES

Ribbing

Multiple of 2+1 sts

Row 1 (RS): K1, (P1, K1) across.

Row 2: Work sts as they appear.

Rep rows 1 and 2 for patt.

Seed stitch in rows

Multiple of 2 sts

Row 1 (RS): (K1, P1) across.

Row 2: Knit the purl sts and purl the knit sts.

Rep rows 1 and 2 for patt.

Seed stitch in the round

Multiple of 2 sts

Rnd 1: (K1, P1) around.

Rnd 2: Knit the purl sts and purl the knit sts.

Rep rnds 1 and 2 for patt.

Cable

See charts A, B, and C (page 83). **Note:** Work sts on WS
rows as they appear.

Pocket Scarf

With straight needles, CO 66 sts and purl 1 row.

Next row (RS): K1 (selvage), work 13 sts seed st, 38 sts
chart A, 13 sts seed st, K1 (selvage).

Work in patt as est until scarf measures 75". BO.

POCKETS

Make 2 alike.

With straight needles, CO 57 sts and purl 1 WS row.

Next row: K1 (selvage), work 14 sts chart B, 27 sts seed
st, 14 sts chart C, K1 (selvage).

Work in patt as est until pocket measures 15¾". Work in
ribbing for 1½". BO.

FINISHING

Weave in ends. Wash pieces and lay flat to dry.

Place the WS of one pocket against the edge of the RS
of the scarf and sew in place.

Rep on opposite end of scarf.

Make 14 pompoms approx 1" in diameter (see
"Pompoms," page 110). Using crochet hook, crochet
chains approx 1" to 2" long and attach a pompom to
one end of each chain. Attach the other end of chain to
the scarf using the photo as a guide.

Hat

The band is worked sideways.

CO 16 sts and work as foll:

Row 1: K1 (selvage), work 14 sts chart B, K1 (selvage). Work in patt, knitting first and last st of each row for selvage sts until piece measures 22". BO.

Sew the CO edge to the BO edge.

With RS facing and dpns, PU 76 sts along one edge of band, PM and join to work in the round. Work in seed st until the hat, including the band, measures 6¼", then dec 8 sts as foll:

Next (dec) rnd: PM after every 19th st. Work in patt as set, working p3tog at each marker—68 sts. Maintaining seed st patt, rep dec rnd every 6th rnd 7 times—12 sts. Work 2 rnds even.

Next rnd: K2tog around—6 sts.

Break yarn, run tail through rem sts. Pull gently to fasten off.

FINISHING

Make 1 pompom (see "Pompoms," page 110) and attach it to the tip of the hat with a 1½" crochet chain.

Weave in ends.

Chart A

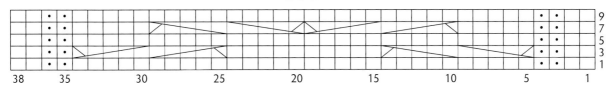

Cable pattern = 38 sts

Chart B

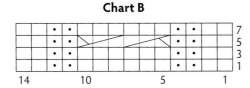

Cable pattern = 14 sts

Chart C

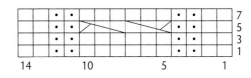

Cable pattern = 14 sts

Chart legend

☐ K on RS, P on WS

• P on RS, K on WS

Sl 3 to cn and hold in back, K3, K3 from cn

Sl 3 to cn and hold in front, K3, K3, from cn

Sl 5 to cn and hold in back, K5, K5 from cn

Sl 5 to cn and hold in front, K5, K5 from cn

Seed Stitch and Cabled Scarf

Skill level: Easy ◼◼☐☐

Size: One size

Finished measurements: Approx 7" x 76"

MATERIALS

Acrylic/wool blend: 300 g/360 yds, color medium gray

Size 11 (8 mm) straight needles or size required to obtain gauge

Cable needle

Tapestry needle

GAUGE

12 sts and 19 rows = 4" in seed st

Cable patt = 2¼" wide

PATTERN STITCHES

Seed stitch

Multiple of 2 sts

Row 1 (RS): (K1, P1) across.

Row 2: Knit the purl sts and purl the knit sts.
Rep rows 1 and 2 for patt.

Cable

Panel of 11 sts

Row 1 (WS): K1 (selvage), P10.

Rows 2–7: Work in St st.

Row 8: Sl 6 sts to cn and hold in front, K5, K6 from cn.

Row 9: K1, P10.

Rows 10–20: Work in St st.

Rep rows 1–20 for patt.

SCARF

CO 26 sts.

Row 1 (WS): Work 11 sts cable panel, 14 sts seed st, K1 (selvage).

Work in patt as est until scarf measures 76", knitting first and last st of each row for selvage. BO.

FINISHING

Weave in ends.

Twisted Cord and Pompoms

Make 2 alike.

Cut 6 pieces of yarn each approx 7 yards long. Make 3 twisted cords as foll:

Holding 2 strands of yarn tog, twist them tightly until they coil back on themselves. Tie ends to secure. Braid these 3 cords together and tie ends to secure. Fold in half and sew to one end of scarf. Make 2 pompoms approx 2" in diameter (see "Pompoms," page 110) and attach to ends of braided cord. Rep on opposite end of scarf.

Blue Cable Wrap

Skill level: Intermediate ■■■□

Size: One size

Finished circumference: Approx 43"

MATERIALS

Wool/acrylic blend: 250 g/670 yds, color indigo ③

Size 6 (4 mm) 29" circular needle or size required to obtain gauge

Stitch marker

Cable needle

Tapestry needle

GAUGE

31 sts and 24 rnds = 4" in cable patt

PATTERN STITCHES

Ribbing

Multiple of 2 sts

All rnds: (K1, P1) around.

Bobble

Worked in 1 st

Row 1: In the next st (K1, YO, K1, YO, K1), turn—5 sts in bobble.

Row 2: Ssk, K1, K2tog, turn—3 sts.

Row 3: P3tog—1 st.

Rep rows 1–3 for each bobble.

Cable

See chart at right. **Note:** Work sts on even-numbered rnds as they appear.

Adjusting Size

This wrap will fit a variety of sizes as written, but if desired, changing the size is easy to do. Simply add or subtract stitches to the cast on amount in multiples of 36, then work pattern as directed. Each multiple of 36 stitches will change the size by approximately 5". Why not 18 stitches to match the chart? The starting bobble round requires a multiple of 4 stitches, and adding just 18 would make it not come out even.

WRAP

CO 324 sts. PM and join to work in the round, being careful not to twist sts.

Rnd 1 (bobble rnd): *K1, P1, K1, make bobble; rep from * around.

Work in ribbing for 2".

Change to cable patt, inc 19 sts in first round as indicated in chart—342 sts.

When piece measures 17¾", change to ribbing, and in the first rnd, K2tog in center of each cable—324 sts rem. Work even until piece measures 19½". BO.

FINISHING

Weave in ends. Wash and lay flat to dry.

Cable chart

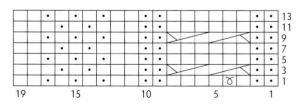

Repeat = 18 increasing to 19 sts

☐ K on RS, P on WS   ⌀ M1

• P on RS, K on WS   ⬚ Sl 3 to cn and hold in back, K3, K3 from cn

Morning Fog

Skill level: Experienced ◼◼◼◗

Size: Women's Average

Finished circumference: Approx 20"

MATERIALS

100% merino wool: 100 g/275 yds, color gray heather
◖3◗

Set of 5 size 4 (3.5 mm) and 6 (4 mm) double-pointed
   needles or size required to obtain gauge

Cable needle

Tapestry needle

GAUGE

22 sts and 32 rows = 4" with larger needles in St st

30 sts and 32 rows = 4" with larger needles in cable patt

PATTERN STITCHES

Ribbing

Multiple of 2 sts

All rnds: (K2, P2) around.

Cable

See chart (page 90). **Note:** Work sts on even-numbered
rnds as they appear.

HAT

With smaller needles, CO 148 sts. Join to work in the
round, being careful not to twist sts. Work in ribbing for
2", in last rnd inc 2 sts—150 sts.

Change to larger needles and beg cable patt.

Beg dec as shown in chart on rnd 41.

At beg of rnd 55, knit first 4 sts, then use those 4 sts
again at end of rnd to work cable.

After rnd 69, 24 sts rem.

FINISHING

Break yarn, run tail through the rem sts and pull gently
to fasten off. Weave in ends.

Cable chart

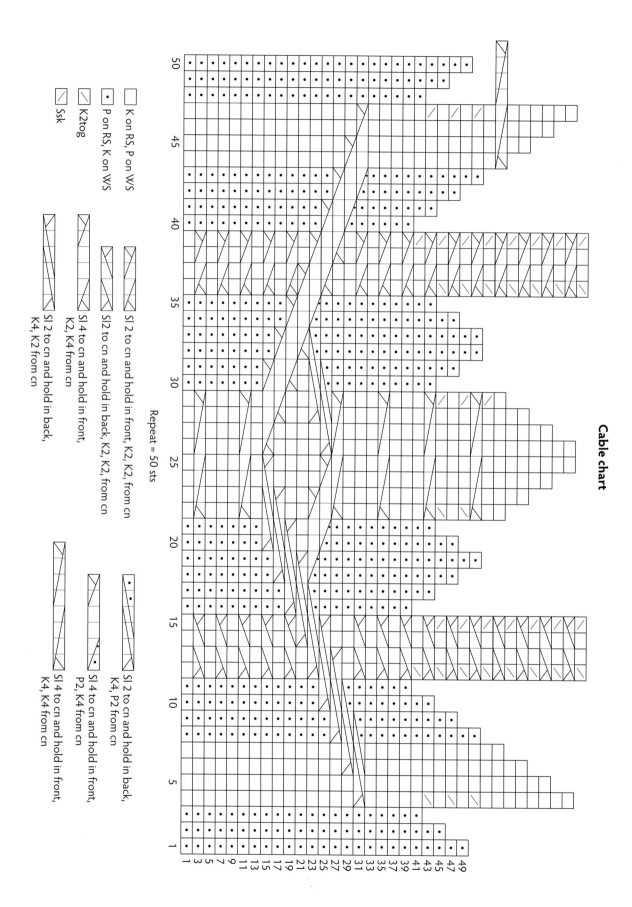

Repeat = 50 sts

K on RS, P on WS

P on RS, K on WS

K2tog

Ssk

Sl 2 to cn and hold in front, K2, K2, K2, from cn

Sl 2 to cn and hold in back, K2, K2, K2, from cn

Sl 4 to cn and hold in front, K2, K4 from cn

Sl 2 to cn and hold in back, K4, K2 from cn

Sl 2 to cn and hold in front, K4, P2 from cn

Sl 4 to cn and hold in front, P2, K4 from cn

Sl 2 to cn and hold in back, K4, K2 from cn

Sl 4 to cn and hold in front, K4, K4 from cn

For Cozy Hours

As an eventful winter day draws to a close, and the weather outside is frightful, it's time to make yourself comfortable inside. Snowflakes floating in front of the window and glittering ice crystals on the glass are an invitation to sit by the crackling fireplace with a cup of hot chocolate and a good book.

Cushy Socks

Skill level: Intermediate ◼◼◼◻

Size: Women's Small/Medium

Finished circumference: 8"

MATERIALS

Wool/nylon blend: 100 g/275 yds, color gray flannel heather ⓷

Set of 5 size 4 (3.5 mm) double-pointed needles or size required to obtain gauge

Cable needle

Tapestry needle

GAUGE

28 sts and 32 rnds = 4" in cable patt

SPECIAL INSTRUCTIONS

C2F: Sl 1 st to cn and hold in front, K1, K1 from cn.

C2B: Sl 1 st to cn and hold in back, K1, K1 from cn.

PATTERN STITCHES

Ribbing

Multiple of 6 sts

All rnds: (P1, K4, P1) around.

Cable

Worked over a multiple of 14 sts.

Note: Always slip sts pw wyib.

Rnd 1: *P1, K4, P2; rep from * around.

Rnds 2–5: *P1, K1, sl 2, K1, P3, sl 1, K2, sl 1, P2; rep from * around.

Rnd 6: *P1, C2B, C2F, P3, C2F, C2B, P2; rep from * around.

Rnd 7: Rep rnd 1.

Rnds 8–11: *P1, sl 1, K2, sl 1, P3, K1, sl 2, K1, P2; rep from * around.

Rnd 12: *P1, C2F, C2B, P3, C2B, C2F, P2; rep from * around.

Rep rnds 1–12 for patt.

SOCKS

Cuff

CO 48 sts. Divide sts evenly over 4 dpns and join to work in the round, being careful not to twist sts (see "Working with Double-Pointed Needles," page 110). Work in ribbing for 3¼".

Next rnd: Inc 2 sts on each needle—8 sts inc, 56 sts total.

Leg

Work cable patt until sock measures 8".

Heel Flap

Turn. Work heel back and forth on 28 sts (leaving other 28 sts on needles on hold) as foll:

Next row (WS): Sl 1, K2 (edge sts), purl to last 3 sts dec 4 sts evenly across, K3 (edge sts)—24 sts rem in heel.

Next row (RS): Sl 1, knit across.

Next row: Sl 1, K2, purl to last 3 sts, K3.

Rep last 2 rows another 10 times.

Turn Heel

Working over 24 heel sts:

Next row (RS): K15, ssk, turn.

Next row (WS): P7, P2tog, turn.

Next row: Sl 1, K6, ssk, turn.

Next row: Sl 1, P6, P2tog, turn.

Rep last 2 rows until 8 sts rem in heel. End after a WS row.

Heel Gusset

With RS facing, set up sts to work in the round as foll:

Needle 1: Work across heel sts, with same needle PU 1 st in each slipped st along side of heel—11 sts PU.

Needles 2 and 3: Work across 28 held instep sts.

Needle 4: PU 1 st in each slipped st along side of heel (11 sts total), K4 to center of heel (new beg of rnd)—58 sts.

Foot

Dec as follows until 56 sts rem:

Rnd 1: Work across needle 1 to last 3 sts, K2tog, K1, work across needles 2 and 3 in cable patt as set; on needle 4, K1, ssk, work to end of rnd.

Rnd 2: Knit.

Work even with instep in cable patt and sole in St st until foot measures 8" or approx 2½" less than desired length.

Toe

Work 4 rnds even in St st.

Dec rnd 1: (K5, K2tog) around—48 sts.

Work 5 rnds even.

Dec rnd 2: (K4, K2tog) around—40 sts.

Work 4 rnds even.

Dec rnd 3: (K3, K2tog) around—32 sts.

Work 3 rnds even.

Dec rnd 4: (K2, K2tog) around—24 sts.

Work 2 rnds even.

Dec rnd 5: (K1, K2tog) around—16 sts.

Work 1 rnd even.

Dec rnd 6: K2tog around—8 sts.

FINISHING

Break yarn, run tail through rem sts.

Weave in ends. Steam or wash socks, and block on sock-blocking forms until dry.

Textured Tunic

Skill level: Easy ◼◼☐☐

Size: Women's Small (Medium, Large)

Finished bust: 38 (41, 44)"

Finished length: 32¾ (32¾, 32¾)"

MATERIALS

100% merino wool: 750 (800, 850) g/1320 (1410, 1495) yds, color dark gray heather (5)

Size 9 (5.5 mm) and 10 (6 mm) straight needles or size required to obtain gauge

Size 9 (5.5mm) 24" circular needle

Stitch markers

Tapestry needle

GAUGE

18 sts and 27 rows = 4" with larger needles in texture patt

PATTERN STITCHES

Ribbing in rows

Multiple of 2+1 sts

Row 1 (RS): K1, (P1, K1) across.

Row 2: Work sts as they appear.

Rep rows 1 and 2 for patt.

Ribbing in the round

Multiple of 2 sts

All rnds: (K1, P1) around.

Texture

Worked over an odd number of sts

Row 1 (RS): Knit.

Row 2: Purl.

Row 3: (P1, K1) to last st, P1.

Row 4: Work sts as they appear.

Rows 5 and 6: Rep rows 1 and 2.

Row 7: (K1, P1) to last st, K1.

Row 8: Work sts as they appear.

Rep rows 1–8 for patt.

BACK

With smaller needles, CO 87 (95, 103) sts and work in ribbing in rows for 3¼". Knit the first and last st of each row for selvage sts.

Change to larger needles and texture patt.

Shape Armholes

When piece measures 22½ (21½, 20¾)" above ribbing, BO 9 sts at beg of next 2 rows—69 (77, 85) sts.

Shape Neck

When piece measures 28" above ribbing, BO center 21 sts, then working each side separately, BO 2 sts at each neck edge twice, then dec 1 st at neck edge once.

When piece measures 32¾" from beg, BO rem 19 (23, 27) sts.

FRONT

Work as for back until piece measures 19" above ribbing.

Shape V-Neck

BO center st (mark this st)—43 (47, 51) sts each side.

Working each side separately, every 4th row, dec 1 st at neck edge 15 times.

Shape Armholes

AT THE SAME TIME, when piece measures same as back to armhole, BO 9 sts at each armhole edge once. When piece measures same as back to shoulders, BO rem 19 (23, 27) sts.

FINISHING

Weave in ends. Wash pieces and lay flat to dry. Sew shoulder seams.

Armhole Bands

With circular needle, PU 67 (75, 83) sts around armhole and work in ribbing in rows for 2". BO loosely in patt.

Rep on other side.

Sew side seams, including edges of bands.

Neckband

With circular needle, RS facing, PU 144 sts around neck opening, PM. Beg at left shoulder, work in ribbing in the round. Every other rnd, work to the st before the marked center st and sl 2tog-K1-P2sso.

When band measures 1¼", BO in patt.

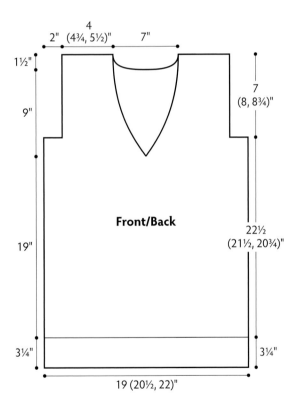

Rest and Relaxation

Lace Pillow

Skill level: Intermediate ◼◼◼☐

Size: One size

Finished measurements: 16" x 16"

MATERIALS

Acrylic/wool/alpaca blend: 100 g/135 yds each of: (6)

  A: light gray

  B: dark gray

Size 10½ (6.5 mm) straight needles or size required to
  obtain gauge

Tapestry needle

16" pillow form

3 buttons, approx 1" diameter

Sewing needle and matching thread

GAUGE

11 sts and 15 rows = 4" in St st

PATTERN STITCHES

Ribbing

Multiple of 2+1 sts

Row 1 (WS): K1, (P1, K1) across.

Row 2: Work sts as they appear.

Rep rows 1 and 2 for patt.

Lace

Panel of 13 sts

Row 1 (RS): K1, K2tog, YO, K2tog, YO, K3, YO, ssk, YO,
ssk, K1.

Rows 2 and 4: Purl.

Row 3: K2, K2tog, YO, K2tog, YO, K1, YO, ssk, YO, ssk, K2.

Rep rows 1–4 for patt.

BUTTON BAND

With B, CO 45 sts and set up ribbing as foll:

Row 1 (WS): K1, (P1, K1) across.

Row 2 (RS): K1 (selvage), work in ribbing as est to last st,
K1 (selvage).

Work in ribbing as set, knitting first and last st of each
row for selvage sts until piece measures 2".

PILLOW

Set up lace panel as foll:

Next row (RS): K1 (selvage), work 15 sts in ribbing,
13 sts of lace panel, 15 sts in ribbing, K1 (selvage).

Work even for 4". Change to color A and work for 22".
Change to B and work for 4" more. End after a WS row.
Piece measures 31".

BUTTONHOLE BAND

With B, work in ribbing for 4 rows.

Next (buttonhole) row (RS): K1, *work 9 sts in ribbing, BO 2 sts; rep from * twice, work 10 sts in ribbing, K1.

Next row: Work patt as est, CO 2 sts over each gap to finish buttonhole. Work even until ribbing measures 2". BO.

FINISHING

Fold the pillow with WS tog and with the buttonhole band folded over to the front to cover the button band (like an envelope). Sew side seams. Weave in ends. Sew buttons opposite buttonholes. Insert the pillow form and button to close.

Smocked Pillow

Skill level: Intermediate ◼◼◼◻
Size: One size
Finished measurements: 16" x 24"

MATERIALS

Acrylic/wool/alpaca blend: 200 g/265 yds, color light gray ⑥

Size 10½ (6.5 mm) straight needles or size required to obtain gauge

Tapestry needle

16" x 24" pillow form

3 buttons, approx 1" diameter

Sewing needle and matching thread

GAUGE

11 sts and 15 rows = 4" in St st
14 sts and 17 rows = 4" in smocking patt

PATTERN STITCHES

Smocking

Multiple of 8+2 sts
Row 1 (RS): P2, *K2, P2; rep from * across.
Row 2: Work sts as they appear.
Row 3: P2, *Smock 1 (insert the needle between the 6th and 7th sts on left needle, pull the yarn through to the front and knit it tog with next st on needle), K1, P2, K2, P2; rep from * across.
Rows 4–6: Work the sts as they appear.
Row 7: P2, K2, P2, *smock 1, K1, P2, K2, P2; rep from * to last 4 sts, K2, P2.
Row 8: Work sts as they appear.
Rep rnds 1–8 for patt.

Trinity

Multiple of 4+2 sts
Row 1 (WS): Purl.
Row 2: K1, *in the next st work (K1, P1, K1), P3tog; rep from * to last st, K1.
Row 3: Purl.
Row 4: K1, *P3tog, in the next st work (K1, P1, K1), rep from * to last st, K1.
Rep rows 1–4 for patt.

Ribbing

Multiple of 2 sts
Row 1 (RS): (K1, P1) across.
Row 2: Work sts as they appear.
Rep rows 1 and 2 for patt.

PILLOW

Left Front

CO 52 sts.

Row 1 (RS): K1 (selvage), work in smocking patt to last st, K1 (selvage). Cont in smocking patt, knitting first and last st for selvage sts, for 12". BO.

Right Front

CO 24 sts.

Row 1 (WS): K1 (selvage), purl to last st, K1 (selvage). Cont in trinity patt, knitting first and last st for selvage sts, for 12". BO.

Back

CO 84 sts. Work as for left front. BO.

FINISHING

With RS facing, PU 48 sts along the right-hand edge of right front and work in ribbing for 2". BO.

Rep on the LH edge of left front, working buttonholes after 4 rows as foll:

Next row: K1 (selvage), *work 10 sts in ribbing, BO 2 sts; rep from * twice, then work 10 sts in ribbing, K1 (selvage). On next row, maintain ribbing patt, CO 2 sts over each gap to finish buttonhole. Work even until ribbing measures 2". BO.

Sew side seams. Weave in ends. Sew buttons opposite buttonholes. Insert pillow form and button to close.

Colorwork Pillow

Skill level: Easy ◼◼☐☐

Size: One size

Finished measurements: 16" x 16"

MATERIALS

Acrylic/wool/alpaca blend: 6

   A: 150 g/200 yds, color light gray

   B: 50 g/66 yds, color dark gray

Size 10½ (6.5 mm) straight needles or size required to obtain gauge

Tapestry needle

16" pillow form

GAUGE

11 sts and 15 rows = 4" in St st

PATTERN STITCHES

Moss

Multiple of 2+1 sts

Row 1 (RS): (K1, P1) across to last st, K1.

Rows 2 and 4: Work sts as they appear.

Row 3: (P1, K1) across to last st, P1.

Rep rows 1–4 for patt.

St st in rows

RS: Knit all sts.

WS: Purl all sts.

Colorwork

See chart at right.

PILLOW

For front, with A, CO 47 sts and *work in moss st for 5". End after a RS row.

Next row (WS): Knit, inc 1 st—48 sts. Work all rows of chart in St st (see "Stranded Colorwork," page 110).

Next row (WS): With A, knit, dec 1 st—47 sts. Work in moss st until piece measures 16". Rep from * for back of pillow. BO.

FINISHING

Fold piece in half and sew side seams. Weave in ends. Insert the pillow form and sew the rem seam closed.

Colorwork chart

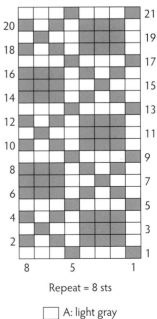

Repeat = 8 sts

☐ A: light gray

▨ B: dark gray

Comfy Dolman-Sleeved Turtleneck

Skill level: Easy ◧■▢▢

Size: Women's Small (Medium, Large)

Finished bust: 36 (39, 43)"

Finished length: 20½ (21¾, 23)"

MATERIALS

100% alpaca: 500 (550, 600) g/1090 (1200, 1310) yds, color lobster ③

Size 6 (4 mm) 32" circular needle and set of 5 double-pointed needles or size required to obtain gauge

Stitch holders

Tapestry needle

GAUGE

18 sts and 35 rows = 4" in texture patt

SPECIAL INSTRUCTIONS

K1 in row below: Insert needle in center of st in row below from front to back, knit the st, dropping st from current row from left needle.

PATTERN STITCHES

Texture

Worked over an odd number of sts

Rows 1, 3, and 5: Knit.

Rows 2 and 4: Purl.

Row 6: *P1, K1 in row below; rep from * across.

Rep rows 1–6 for patt.

Ribbing

Multiple of 6 sts.

All rnds: (K3, P3) around.

BACK

With circular needle, CO 85 (91, 99) sts. Work in texture patt until piece measures 6¾", knitting first and last st of each row for selvage sts. End after a WS row.

Shape Armholes

Inc 1 st each end of row every RS row 22 (23, 24) times as foll:

Inc row (RS): K2, YO, work in patt to last 2 sts, YO, K2—129 (137, 147) sts.

Shape Shoulders

Work even until piece measures 12¼ (13¾, 13¾)". End after a WS row.

Dec 1 st each end of row every RS row 36 (40, 45) times as foll:

Dec row (RS): K2, ssk, work to last 4 sts, K2tog, K2—57 sts.

Work even until piece measures 20½ (21¾, 23)", put rem sts on hold for neck.

FRONT

Work as for back.

SLEEVES

Make 2 alike.

With circular needle, CO 57 (63, 71) sts. Work in texture patt until piece measures 11½ (10¾, 10)". BO.

FINISHING

Weave in ends. Wash piece and lay flat to dry. Sew shoulder seams, sew sleeves to shoulders, sew underarm and side seams.

NECKBAND

With dpns, RS facing, work across the 57 neck sts on both pieces—114 sts total. Work in ribbing for 8". BO loosely in patt. Fold collar in half to outside.

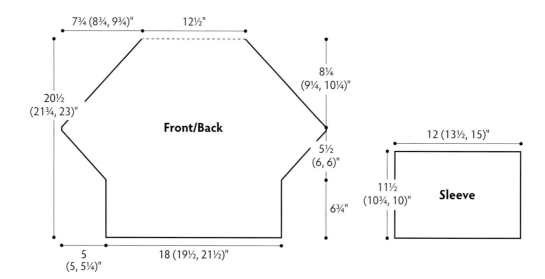

Comfy Dolman-Sleeved Turtleneck

Basic and Special Knitting Techniques

This section explains the basic knitting techniques you'll need to guarantee success in knitting the projects in this book, from casting on to making the basic stitches, to binding off and finishing seams. Some projects also employ special techniques, such as color knitting, working short rows, or embellishing garments with fringes or pompoms. These are also explained in this section. To make it easy for you to find the information you need, each pattern lists any special techniques and tells you where you'll find the instructions. With the basics under your belt, nothing will be more fun than knitting!

CASTING ON

Long Tail Cast On

1. To make the first stitch, take the yarn from the center of the ball and pull out a tail approx 3 times the width of the piece you'll be knitting. Hold the tail of the yarn in your left hand and the working yarn and needle in your right hand.

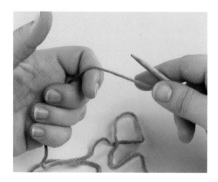

2. Wrap the yarn clockwise around your left thumb.

3. Insert the needle into the loop on your thumb from bottom to top.

4. Take your thumb out of the yarn and pull the yarn tight around the needle so the strands cross under the needle.

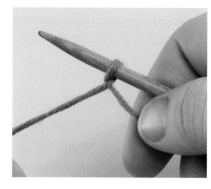

5. With the loop for the first stitch on the needle, place the working yarn around your left index finger and the yarn tail around your left thumb. Grasp the strands in your palm with your little finger and ring finger.

6. Pull the needle down a bit, until the two parts of the thumb yarn cross, and insert the needle from below into thumb loop.

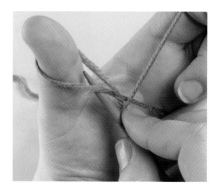

7. Draw the working yarn through the loop, then pull your thumb out of the loop.

8. You now have another stitch on the needle. Reposition your thumb under the tail and your index finger under the working yarn, and tug gently to tighten the new stitch on the needle. Repeat the process until you have cast on the desired number of stitches.

Cable Cast On

Some projects require a very large number of stitches to be cast on, so it becomes cumbersome to draw out a long tail of yarn to begin. At other times, such as when creating buttonholes, you need to cast on in the middle of a row. In these two situations, it is best to use a cable cast on.

1. *With the right needle, insert the tip of the needle between the first two stitches on the left needle.

2. Place the new stitch onto the left needle, pulling out a fairly large loop so the stitches will not be too tight. Do not tighten the new stitch until you insert the needle again to create the following stitch. Repeat from *, always knitting into the last stitch made.

Provisional Cast On

A few of the projects in this book call for a provisional cast on. While there are a few ways to work a provisional cast on, this is one of the easiest. You'll need waste yarn in a contrasting color (smooth yarn in the same or slightly lighter weight works best) and a crochet hook approximately the same size as your needles.

With crochet hook and waste yarn, crochet a chain a bit longer than the number of stitches to cast on. Fasten off.

With needles and project yarn, pick up and knit 1 stitch in each chain until the desired number of stitches is cast on. Leave a few chains empty on each end to make it easier to undo the chain later.

When directed, undo the end of the chain and carefully unravel it, exposing the live stitches. Place the stitches one at a time on the needles as the chain unravels. Finish live stitches as pattern indicates.

KNIT STITCH

1. With the working yarn in *back* of the left needle, insert the right needle under the left needle and into the first stitch *from front to back.*

2. Pull the yarn through the loop on the left needle.

3. Drop the old stitch from the left needle.

Stockinette Stitch

One of the basic stitches in knitting, called stockinette stitch, is made by alternating between a row of knitting (the right side of the work) and a row of purling (the wrong side of the work).

Garter Stitch

The most basic stitch in knitting, called garter stitch, is made by knitting every row (both right-side and wrong-side rows), which creates a reversible fabric.

PURL STITCH

1. With the working yarn in *front* of the needle, insert the right needle into the first stitch *from back to front.* Wrap the working yarn around the right needle counterclockwise.

2. Use your index finger to pull the yarn down in front of the work, making it easier to draw the yarn through the stitch on the left needle.

3. Pull the yarn through, and then drop the old stitch from the left needle.

Reverse Stockinette Stitch

Alternating between a row of purling (on the right side) and a row of knitting (on the wrong side) is called reverse stockinette stitch.

SELVAGE STITCHES

Always work a special selvage stitch at the beginning and end of every row to make it easier to sew pieces together. All of the projects in this book are worked with selvage stitches. There are many different ways to work a selvage stitch, but for simplicity's sake we specified a garter stitch selvage for most of the projects. Here are three; feel free to choose the one that you prefer.

Garter stitch selvage: When you knit the first and last stitch of every row, this forms little knots along the edges of the knitting. This makes a very nice border when the edges of the fabric will not be hidden in seams.

Seam selvage: When you knit the first and last stitch of every RS row and purl the first and last stitch of every WS row, this forms a stockinette stitch selvage that you may find easier to use when sewing seams.

Chain selvage: When you slip the first stitch of every row, this creates a smooth chain going up the edge of the fabric. This is used on the side edges of a sock heel.

PUTTING STITCHES ON HOLD

Sometimes you'll need to put stitches on hold to be worked later. This may happen when you're knitting a garment in several pieces that will be put together later. For example, when knitting the back of a sweater, you may be instructed to put the neck stitches on a holder rather than binding them off. After knitting the front of the sweater, the shoulders are joined and then the stitches on holders are used to knit the neckband. On socks, after you work the leg of the sock, half of the stitches are put on holders while you work the heel of the sock, then you come back to work all of the stitches again later, after the heel has been finished. You can put the held stitches on a stitch holder, a length of scrap yarn, or a spare needle. The spare needle does not need to be the same size as the needles used for the project.

INCREASES AND DECREASES

Make 1 (M1, increase). With the tip of the left needle, lift the strand between the last stitch worked and the next stitch on the needle. Place the strand onto the left needle. Knit into the *back* of the newly created loop to "make one" stitch.

Make 1

Knit two together (K2tog, decrease). The *knit two together (K2tog) decrease* removes one stitch from your knitting. This decrease slants to the right. Insert the needle through *two loops* on the left needle at once, and work them together as a regular knit stitch.

Knit 2 together

Slip-slip-knit (ssk, decrease). To make a mirror-image decrease that slants to the left, use a *slip-slip-knit (ssk)* decrease. Slip the next two stitches one at a time to the right needle *as if to knit*. Insert the left needle into the front of the stitches and knit the two stitches together through the back loops with the right needle.

Purl two together (P2tog, decrease). On wrong-side rows or when the pattern instructs, you may need to purl two stitches together.

Purl 2 together

BINDING OFF

This bind off is worked as a regular row, with each stitch being eliminated after it is worked. The advantage to this technique is that you can bind off "in pattern"—that is, you can either knit or purl each stitch before eliminating it.

1. Starting on a RS row, knit (or purl) one stitch. *Work another stitch. You now have two stitches on the right needle.

2. Insert the left needle into the second stitch on the right needle, and pass it over the first, dropping it off the needles. One stitch remains on the right needle.
   Repeat from * until you have bound off all stitches.

PICKING UP STITCHES

To attach a new section of knitting to an existing piece, you must *pick up stitches* along the edge of your knitting.

1. Insert the needle into the center of the stitch just inside the selvage of your knitting.

2. Pull the yarn through. You have picked up one stitch. Repeat these steps to pick up the required number of stitches.

3. In most cases, you will be picking up approximately three out of every four stitches along the edge of a piece of knitting.

STRANDED COLORWORK

Knitting with two colors in a row to form color patterns that reach all the way across your knitting is called stranded knitting, also known as Fair Isle or jacquard knitting. When knitting with two colors in a row, you should weave the unused color as you go. This prevents the yarns from tangling and creates a smooth, neat back for your knitting.

1. Working with both hands, hold the main color in your right hand (English style) and the contrast color in your left hand (Continental style). Lift the index finger of your left hand so the yarn held there (the non-working yarn) is *above* the working yarn, and knit the next one or two stitches with the working yarn. Move the yarn in your left hand *below* the working yarn, and knit the next stitch normally with the working yarn.

2. The non-working yarn will be woven in on the wrong side. Weave the non-working yarn every few stitches to avoid long floats.

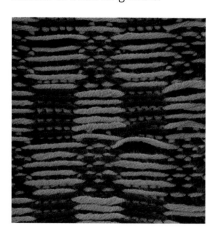

3. Both yarns can also be held in the left hand as you work.

WORKING WITH DOUBLE-POINTED NEEDLES

In this book, socks, as well as the collars on some sweaters, are worked with sets of five double-pointed needles, with the stitches divided equally on four needles and the fifth needle used for knitting. The needles are numbered clockwise starting from the beginning of the round.

Start by casting on. You'll need to join the stitches into a circle without twisting them. An easy way to do this is to place the needles on a flat surface and make sure all the stitches are lined up on the inside of the curve of the needles. With the tail and the working yarn on the right-hand needle, carefully pick up the needles and knit the first couple of stitches. This completes your join. The tail of the yarn can function as a marker to indicate the beginning of the round.

FRINGE

A basic fringe is made by adding strands of yarn evenly spread out across the ends of a knitted piece. Cut two to four strands of yarn to twice the length of the finished fringe, and fold in half. Insert a crochet hook through the edge of the piece and draw up a loop from the center of the folded fringe. Pull the ends of the fringe strands through the folded loop and tug gently on the ends to secure. Trim even if desired.

POMPOMS

1. Cut two doughnut-shaped pieces out of cardboard, and cut off several strands of yarn approximately two yards long.

2. Place the rings together and wind the yarn around the rings.

3. When all of the cardboard is covered, use scissors to cut around the edge using the division between the two pieces of cardboard as a guide.

4. Pass a strand of yarn between the pieces of cardboard, wrapping it around the center of the pompom, and tie it firmly together.

5. Remove the cardboard and trim the yarn to shape pompom.

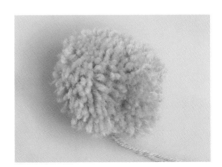

MATTRESS STITCH

With the right sides facing up, place the two pieces to be seamed on a flat surface. With a tapestry needle and matching yarn, go under the one or two bars between the selvage stitch and the next stitch near the edge of one piece of knitting. Repeat on the other piece.

Continue to work from side to side, pulling gently on the yarn to close the seam every 2".

GAUGE

To measure gauge, work a swatch at least 4" x 4" in the pattern stitch indicated for the selected project.

Cast on about 20 to 24 stitches and work until you have about 5" of knitting. If your stitch gauge is not exact, your garment will not come out the size indicated in the pattern.

To measure the stitch gauge, place a ruler or tape measure across your swatch horizontally. Mark the beginning and end of 4" and count the stitches:

On garter stitch, count the bumps on the top of the row.

On stockinette stitch, count the Vs formed by the stitches.

To measure the row gauge, place a ruler or tape measure across your swatch vertically. Mark the beginning and end of 4" with pins or masking tape. Count the rows. If the number of stitches and rows in your swatch is more than recommended, try again with a smaller needle. If you have fewer stitches and rows than recommended, try a larger needle.

Abbreviations

approx	approximately	kw	knitwise	RH	right hand
beg	begin(ning)	LH	left hand	rnd(s)	round(s)
BO	bind off	M1	make 1 stitch (see page 108)	RS	right side
CC	contrasting color	MC	main color	sc	single crochet
cn	cable needle	mm	millimeter	sl	slip
CO	cast on	oz	ounces	sl st	slip stitch
cont	continue(ing)	P	purl	ssk	slip, slip, knit (see page 109)
dec	decrease(s)(ing)	patt	pattern	sssk	slip, slip, slip knit
dpn(s)	double-pointed needle(s)	PM	place marker	st(s)	stitch(es)
est	established	psso	pass slipped stitch over	St st	stockinette stitch
foll	following	P2tog	purl 2 stitches together (see page 109)	tbl	through back loop
g	grams			WS	wrong side
inc	increase(s)(ing)	P3tog	purl 3 stitches together	wyib	with yarn in back
K	knit	PU	pick up and knit	wyif	with yarn in front
K2tog	knit 2 stitches together (see page 109)	pw	purlwise	yd(s)	yard(s)
K3tog	knit 3 stitches together	rem	remain(ing)	YO	yarn over
		rep(s)	repeat(s)		

Useful Information

METRIC CONVERSIONS

Yards x .91 = meters

Meters x 1.09 = yards

Grams x .035 = ounces

Ounces x 28.35 = grams

STANDARD YARN-WEIGHT SYSTEM

Yarn-Weight Symbol and Category Names	Super Fine 1	Fine 2	Light 3	Medium 4	Bulky 5	Super Bulky 6
Types of Yarns in Category	Sock, Fingering, Baby	Sport, Baby	DK, Light Worsted	Worsted, Afghan, Aran	Chunky, Craft, Rug	Bulky, Roving
Knit Gauge Ranges in Stockinette Stitch to 4"	27 to 32 sts	23 to 26 sts	21 to 24 sts	16 to 20 sts	12 to 15 sts	6 to 11 sts
Recommended Needle in US Size Range	1 to 3	3 to 5	5 to 7	7 to 9	9 to 11	11 and larger
Recommended Needle in Metric Size Range	2.25 to 3.25 mm	3.25 to 3.75 mm	3.75 to 4.5 mm	4.5 to 5.5 mm	5.5 to 8 mm	8 mm and larger